One Woman's Jihad

One Woman's Jihad

Nana Asma'u
Scholar and Scribe

Beverly B. Mack and Jean Boyd

INDIANA UNIVERSITY PRESS
BLOOMINGTON & INDIANAPOLIS

This book is a publication of
Indiana University Press
601 North Morton Street
Bloomington, IN 47404-3797 USA

http://www.indiana.edu/~iupress
Telephone orders   800-842-6796
Fax orders   812-855-7931
Orders by e-mail   iuporder@indiana.edu

The paper used in this publication meets the minimum requirements
of American National Standard for Information Sciences—Permanence of Paper for Printed Library Materials, ANSI Z39.48-1984.

Manufactured in the United States of America

Library of Congress Cataloging-in-Publication Data

Mack, Beverly B. (Beverly Blow), date
     One woman's Jihad : Nana Asma'u, scholar and scribe / Beverly B.
Mack and Jean Boyd.
        p.   cm.
     Includes bibliographical references and index.
     ISBN 0-253-33707-0 (cloth : alk. paper)—ISBN 0-253-21398-3
(paper : alk. paper)
         1. Asma'u, Nana, 1793–1865. 2. Women authors, Hausa—
Biography. 3. Fulani Empire—Biography. 4. Muslim women—
Fulani Empire—Biography. I. Boyd, Jean. II. Title.

PL8234.A85 Z77 2000
297.8'1'092—dc21
[B]
                                                              99-053817
       3   4   5   6   7   11   10   09   08   07   06

To my family, who have supported me, always. J.B.

❀

To Bob, Tom, and Sarah. B.B.M.

❀

Thanks to Allan Christelow for the title. B.B.M. *and* J.B.

Contents

Contents

Preface

How I "Found" Asma'u

Asma'u, daughter of Shehu ɗan Fodiyo, is best known by her name and honorific: Nana Asma'u. She has been famous throughout West Africa for more than 150 years, although very few people are able to describe exactly what she did. Like all other British expatriates in Nigeria, I had no knowledge of her when I landed on that country's shores in 1955 as a newly recruited woman education officer in the British Colonial Service. I was posted to Katsina to teach at the Provincial Girls School. The girls, who ranged in age from eight to twelve, had been drafted in to provide future entrants to the only girls' secondary school in the north, which was situated five hundred miles away in Ilorin.

The history we taught was about the coming of the Europeans. Even at secondary-school level, the textbook in use, *The House of History,* was the same as that being used in English grammar schools in the 1930s, it being deemed "reactionary and lacking in vision" to study indigenous or Islamic history. This was patently wrong, but no one did anything. All around us there was evidence of layers of historical development which we teachers knew nothing about. In 1963, when I found that children were being taught about David Livingstone in the nearby school, I thought it was time to do something, so I collected stories about Katsina history. My mentor was the Wali of Katsina, Alhaji Muhammad Bello, who translated Arabic documents for me.

It quickly became clear that all paths led to Sokoto as far as nineteenth-century history was concerned, so when we returned to live there in 1967, I started to quarry the history of the area, without knowing any Arabic but with a fair degree of fluency in Hausa. I was a total amateur. The watershed historical event of the region was the Sokoto jihad (1804–30), which had been led by Shehu Usman ɗan Fodiyo. What set my imagination going was a visit to the site of the Battle of Tabkin Kwatto, the turning point of the jihad, and the victory likened by Asma'u's father, the Shehu, to the Prophet Muhammad's victory at Badr. I did not know these things when I got into a Land Rover and motored down corrugated roads and along field tracks to Kwatto. In the simple unroofed mosque I saw the stakes which the victors had driven into the ground in 1804 to ensure that the place was never forgotten.

I found this exciting and wanted to write about it. I wanted the children I was teaching to know and value their past. Anxious to learn more, I asked one of the teachers at my school, Sidi Sayudi, now a *qadi* (judge), if he could translate a short paragraph from a book called *Infaq al-maisur* by Caliph Muhammad Bello. This led to our decision to translate the whole of *Infaq* into Hausa, a project which would in turn lead directly to my involvement with Nana Asma'u.

However, we quickly ran into difficulties. There were no maps with the text, and we didn't know with any degree of precision where many of the places were; here we are not talking of major towns but rocky outcrops, tributary rivers, watering holes, ancient abandoned villages and campsites. Over a two-year period we visited the places mentioned in *Infaq* using transport usually provided by the present Sultan, Alhaji Muhammad Maccido, who was then Sarkin Kudu of Sokoto. He also informed people of our coming, which meant we were welcomed.

It was a fascinating thing to have done, and it certainly could not be done today in the same way because roads and dams have changed the countryside. Our hosts were always the local dignitaries: they provided the accommodation, food, and informants. We sat on mats in halls lit by kerosene lamps listening to old men's recollections, climbed precipitous hills to reach walled fortresses, crossed swollen rivers in leaky dugout canoes, drove deep into the Saharan fringes to view Dutsen Zana, the Hill of Disappearance. Over one Christmas the entire family became involved when we journeyed for days to reach Tafadek, where there are hot springs in a desert place and where the Shehu had lived for a year.

During the whole of this time I knew only a little about Nana Asma'u, but I did become a student of her descendant, the famous

Waziri of Sokoto Alhaji Dr. Junaidu. Waziri Junaidu took a personal interest in the translation of *Infaq* and made the final corrections in the typescript. We met with him on numerous occasions in his house and it was there I asked him about Nana Asma'u. I told him that I understood that she had written five poems in Arabic and requested that he lend me copies of them. "Five?" he queried, "Are you sure?" He left the room to return holding aloft a *gafaka*, or goatskin satchel, which contained his collection of her works written on old yellowing paper. There were not only the poems in Arabic but all the rest written in Fulfulde and Hausa. He gave me the *gafaka*, which held many more than five poems.

I photocopied the works and returned the originals to the *Waziri*. I then had handwritten copies made of each document, a process that took months. Meanwhile I learned to read Arabic script and then acted as an amanuensis, writing down in Hausa roman script the translations from the Arabic and Fulfulde and the transliterations from the Hausa poems which had been previously written down in Arabic script. The experts—the *Waziri*, Malam Sidi Sayuɗi, and a Fulfulde-speaking scholar called Malam Muhammadu Magaji—worked with me on this project for years. We made no attempt to translate the texts into English, concentrating instead on the complex issues of interpretation. To understand a poem about a battle, one had to know what the rules of engagement were. To find out about these, the books written on warfare by Asma'u's contemporaries had to be studied, books which one couldn't get from a bookshop and which were in Arabic. To explore matters such as medicine, gender relationships, tax collection, the structure of government, and friendships took years, especially as we all had full-time jobs: the *Waziri* was the Sultan's chief adviser, Malam Sidi was a judge, Malam Muhammadu had his business interests in cattle, and I was a head teacher.

I had the privilege of visiting the room where Nana Asma'u lived and worked, and of interviewing scores of women who were descended from the students she taught in the period 1830–63. I rode on horseback where she had ridden in 1804, listening to the wind blow through the guineacorn and watching the birds by the river. With a donkey to carry my loads and two brilliant horsemen at my side in case of disaster, I reached my destination at Alƙalawa believing that I had seen something of what she had seen.

On one of his visits to our home, Professor Murray Last advised me to register for a higher degree in England and promised to supervise my studies. In 1982, before leaving Nigeria finally, I submitted a master's thesis on Asma'u. We left Nigeria for the last time in 1984. After that I developed ten radio programs about Asma'u which were broadcast in Hausa on the World Service of the BBC, and my thesis was published in 1989 as a biography of Asma'u called *The Caliph's Sister*. Meanwhile, I had been seeking a suitable home for my collected research notes and papers on Asma'u. The archivist from the library at the School of Oriental and African Studies came to assess the collection and accepted it on loan. In addition, I took the documents to the British Library, where I had the manuscripts copied as microfiches, each work alongside its Hausa translation. One microfiche found its way to Yale. At this point I believed that I had done all I could with Asma'u's papers. What I have written here tells how I "found" Nana Asma'u. What happened after that is another story involving Beverly Mack.

J.B.
Penrith, Cumbria
June 1999

In 1979 I went to the city of Kano in northern Nigeria on a Fulbright doctoral dissertation grant to find, record, and analyze Hausa women's praise poetry. The male royal praise poets had by then been the subject of M. G. Smith's anthropological studies, but no one had studied the women praise poets of the Emir of Kano, presumably because few Western women had embarked on research in the region, and it took another woman to mingle with Muslim women in the privacy of their homes. In the research process the study broadened to include not only extemporaneous praise poets of the royal court, but also literate women poets versed in the Arabic literary tradition. In the course of graduate studies I had learned of Shehu Usman dan Fodiyo, but heard nothing of women's roles in nineteenth-century Hausa-Fulani history. It is extraordinary that nothing had been published about Nana Asma'u or her works either in Nigeria or here in the West. In Nigeria

Asma'u was a legendary figure among women, but there were no books about her; she had no official place in history. As an outsider, I had no means of knowing about Asma'u, so I was surprised when an indignant Hausa woman poet challenged, "How can you ask whether I have my husband's permission to write? Did Nana Asma'u ever need her husband's permission? Go to Sokoto and find Jean Boyd. She will show you Nana Asma'u!" Obedient to her command, I made the pilgrimage across hundreds of miles of arid savannah to find a twentieth-century woman whose name had come to be linked with Nana Asma'u's. In Sokoto I asked the first person I saw where I might find Jean Boyd. I was led to her house, and introduced myself. When I said I had come to look for Nana Asma'u, Jean said I was about a century and a half too late, and invited me in for tea.

Our conversation that day revealed that Jean had been working with Asma'u's poems for many years, and despite the immense corpus of the works, progress had been made. There were, after all, many years of historical context to be accounted for, and several layers of language to unravel in the transformations of the works from one language to another. Asma'u was multilingual, like all accomplished scholars of her time. She had composed works in three languages: Arabic, Fulfulde, and Hausa, all written in the Arabic script. British colonial rule in the twentieth century brought roman script to the region, and since the 1920s Hausa has been written in that Western form, while Arabic and Fulfulde remain for the most part rendered in Arabic script. Jean's translations of Asma'u's poems were from the Arabic script versions of three languages into what had become the predominant language, Hausa, and the predominant form, roman script. As a researcher I was simultaneously thrilled and dismayed at this discovery. I was thrilled to know of Asma'u's works, and dismayed to have no access to the works as a comparative reference. I had a strong intuitive sense of Asma'u's relevance to the contemporary poets I was studying, and was eager to compare their works with Asma'u's. Since I knew Hausa, I was able to read them, but the "Asma'u papers" were still in Jean's home, and still inaccessible to scholars. The best I could do was to encourage Jean to make the material available by publishing it somehow. Her long residence in Nigeria was coming to an end, and my research drew me back to Kano. I saw Jean and her husband once more before they left for England in 1984. By the mid-1980s Jean had donated her notes, comprehensive catalogues of the works, and the poems themselves to the University of London School for Oriental and African Studies archives, where they were stored on microfiche.

By 1986 I was teaching at Yale University, and had just procured Jean's microfiche catalogue of the collection. Microfiche are themselves difficult to read, and the massive body of material was nearly impossible for the uninitiated to use effectively. Trained in literary analysis and historical method, I wanted to use the works themselves, in versions as close to the originals as possible, as a context for my own work on contemporary women's poetry. I contacted Jean and asked whether she would consider putting them together in a volume of English translations with extensive notes for those newly acquainted with Nana Asma'u. The thought of translating to English thousands of lines of poetry that span Asma'u's entire lifetime was daunting. We both realized it would be a formidable task, taking a number of years, but fortunately we had no idea of the true magnitude of work that lay ahead. To this end, I wrote and won for us a collaborative grant from the National Endowment for the Humanities that supported us both for two years, full-time, to work together on the project now published as *The Collected Works of Nana Asma'u, 1793–1864* (1997). That 753-page book represents what Asma'u held in her head. Whenever the computer crashed (I wore out a hard drive on this project) and we wanted to give up, we realized that quitting was not an option our subject would allow; Asma'u's fortitude and productivity in the face of hardship inspired or shamed us into seeing the project through to the end.

Ironically, when that book was done, we realized we still were not finished, because the text and translation tome was insufficiently accessible to average students. We felt they should know about Asma'u, a nineteenth-century Muslim woman who defies contemporary stereotypes, and who typifies the ideal of the scholarly, pious, and yet worldly woman. Asma'u helped transform her society by resocializing war refugees and contributed significantly to the Islamic reformation process in northern Nigeria. She has long been a role model for Hausa-Fulani women, and continues to be *to this very day*. Her formidable literary legacy represents but a portion of the effect she had in reshaping her society. Now at last, I am able to return to the Hausa women's poetry of my dissertation and put it into historical context, understanding why and how contemporary Hausa women poets consider Asma'u their mentor.

B.B.M.
Lawrence, Kansas
June 1999

Acknowledgments

We are grateful to many colleagues for their interest in and comments on this book as it was evolving, and we thank the University of Kansas Hall Center for the Humanities for funding the creation of the index. The Waziri of Sokoto, Alhaji Dr. Junaidu, Malam Sidi Sayu'di, and Malam Muhammadu Magaji were central to the long and arduous process of opening Asma'u's works to the world beyond Sokoto. Many others also have been instrumental along the way, especially Professor Murray Last at University College, London, and the twentieth-century Hausa women poets in Kano who inspired further investigation into Asma'u's work. Beyond these contemporaries, it is obvious that Nana Asma'u herself is the inspiration for this volume. It is our hope that her work will be the source of many other scholarly and creative works linking Muslim West Africa with the rest of the world, and spreading the news of Muslim women's innumerable contributions to their societies.

Note on Foreign Terms

Many Arabic terms have become a part of the Hausa language, in which a glottal stop is marked in roman script by an apostrophe. Because this book focuses on works in Hausa, glottal stops for vowels are marked in this way. Ayns and hamzas are not distinguished in the Arabic terms used here, but are indicated only by an apostrophe. The name 'Ayesha appears in *The Collected Works of Nana Asma'u* in its Arabic form. It has been changed here to its Hausa form—Aisha—for consistency in both the text and the appendix.

The Hausa language has several "hooked" letters that are known as glottalized consonants. These include ɓ, ɗ, ƙ, and 'y (in uppercase Ɓ, Ɗ, Ƙ, and 'Y), and are distinct from the letters b, d, k, and y. Throughout this text, such letters represent glottal sounds and are shown in both upper- and lowercase, as designated above. Hausa also tends to add the vowel "u" to many terms: Asma/Asma'u, Muhammad/Muhammad'u.

Throughout the text, foreign words are always italicized. Their origin is given only the first time they appear, and only when they are not Hausa terms. The glossary is a listing of Hausa and other foreign terms. The origin of certain terms is given when the word (usually Arabic) does not appear in the Hausa lexicon. Otherwise it is treated as a Hausa term.

The term "jihad" is often understood in the West to mean "holy war," yet its real meaning is simply "struggle." It is known by Arabic speakers to refer to the greatest struggle of humankind, which is to be less attached to the world and more attached to God. Upon returning from battle, the Prophet Muhammad is known to have said, "We have left the lesser jihad, and returned to the greater jihad," implying that the battle to perfect the self is far more difficult than fighting an enemy on the battlefield. Asma'u's life was a struggle to promote understanding of God, which she accomplished through her life's work as a teacher. Therefore, we have chosen to call her life's work a "jihad" in reference to the literal meaning of the term: a struggle to promote acceptance of the will of God.

One Woman's Jihad

Nana Asma'u and the Scholarly Islamic Tradition

One This book focuses on a nineteenth-century Muslim woman in West Africa who was a legend in her own time. Nana Asma'u (1793–1864) was a respected public figure of significant authority. She was active in politics, education, and social reform; she was a prolific author, popular teacher, and renowned scholar and intellectual. Asma'u did not accomplish her work in isolation; she was actively involved with her family and the wider community of which it was a part. She managed a household of several hundred in an age when technology was restricted to what could be rendered by hand for the growth, production, and processing of food or material goods. During warfare, she was an eyewitness to battles about which she reported in her written works. Throughout the period of the Sokoto jihad, a series of battles in a campaign to reform Islam (1804–1830), and long after, Asma'u was an active teacher of both men and women. In addition to teaching students in her own community, she reached far beyond the confines of her compound through a network of itinerant women teachers whom she trained to teach isolated rural women. An accomplished author, Asma'u was well educated, quadrilingual (in Arabic, Fulfulde, Hausa, and Tamachek), and a respected scholar of international repute who was in communication with scholars throughout the sub-Saharan African Muslim world. Asma'u pursued all these endeavors as a Sufi of the Qadiriyya order, but the driving factor in her own life and that of the community was their concern for the *Sunna,* the exemplary way of life set forth by the Prophet Muhammad. With the *Sunna* orchestrating the lives of its members, Asma'u's Qadiriyya community sought to serve through teaching, preaching, and practical work, focused on a spiritual life in the world, while rejecting materialism.

Asma'u was a pearl on a string of women's scholarship that extended throughout the Muslim world. This chain of women scholars originated long before Asma'u's lifetime and stretched over a wide geographic region from the Middle East to West Africa.[1] The network of women's scholarship contemporaneous to Asma'u is but the tip of the iceberg. It did not spring forth full-blown, but was nurtured over successive generations as an integral part of the aim of Islam: the search for communion with God through the pursuit of Truth. Education and literacy have been hallmarks of Islam since its inception. Any society that impedes equitable access to salvation by controlling or limiting who can get an education eschews the tenets of Islam; so for the Qadiriyya community to which Asma'u belonged, to deny women equal opportunity to develop their God-given talents was to challenge God's will.

This book has two aims. The first is to bring to life a nineteenth-century Muslim West African woman of renown. There is no doubt that Nana Asma'u was exemplary in her character and accomplishments. Her story speaks for itself, without question. The second aim is to suggest that there may be women in other Sufi communities bordering the Sahara who also performed an important part in their societies. Nana Asma'u is exceptional in her achievements but may not be unique in the role she played. This task can be only begun here, by motivating readers to seek further sources in other languages and other places, and mine them more deeply.

Historical Background

Centuries prior to Nana Asma'u's birth, fortressed cities of the region of what is now northwestern Nigeria (see map) had been thriving as commercial and religious centers. To their urban Hausa inhabitants, trans-Saharan commerce was common; these cities were entrepôts for both material and human goods, with slave-raiding long an integral part of life. When trans-Saharan commercial caravans reached Kano in the fourteenth century A.D., the city's fifty-foot-tall gates in the twenty-five-foot-thick city walls opened to welcome them. Islam had been introduced into the area as early as the fourteenth century, brought from both the west and the north by Fulani clerics and Arab, Dyula, and Wangarawa traders. The Fulani were commonly seen in cities such as Kano, Zaria, Daura, and Katsina, and they often settled down and contributed to the region's cosmopolitan culture, which was increasingly Islamic in nature.[2] The literacy of Muslim traders was an integral part of their Qur'anic study. For the successful urban merchant wishing to do international business, literacy and numeracy were as essential as knowledge of Islamic culture. Throughout urban centers of the region, commercial relations among Hausa, Fulani, and North African cultures fostered a shared understanding whose philosophical foundation was Islam.

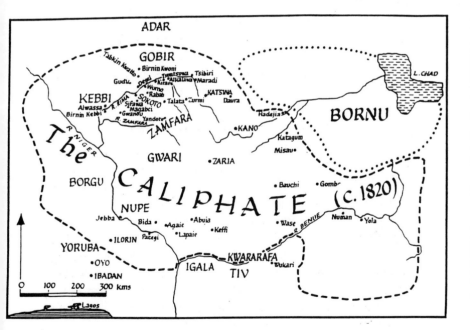

Figure 1.1. The Sokoto Caliphate, circa 1820, showing fortressed cities

By the late eighteenth century, the majority of people in northern Nigeria identified themselves with Islam, and even those who did not would have recognized a Muslim at prayer and heard the call to prayer punctuating the day's activities at regular intervals. Yet there was little to compel unbelievers to become practicing Muslims, because non-Muslim traditions were protected and promoted. The old religion based on spirit possession flourished. Nevertheless, the long-standing presence of Islam throughout the area meant that when the Shehu began preaching, he was renewing and purifying an integral part of the culture, not starting from scratch.[3]

In 1793, the year of Asma'u's birth in the rural region now known as northwestern Nigeria, settlements of Hausa and Fulani people populated the area where Asma'u and her family lived. The area is savannah, with tall-grass prairies, ideal for grazing cattle and raising grain crops. The Hausa and the Fulani had lived in the region for centuries, the Hausa as indigenes, and the Fulani having migrated eastward over successive generations from points of ethnic origin in Senegal and Guinea. The Hausa were agriculturalists, craftspeople, and traders. The majority of the Fulani were cattle herders, some tended sheep and goats, while a few had become Islamic scholars, following vocations of teaching, and sometimes offering their skills to non-literate elite in the urban areas.

The Beginnings of the Sokoto Jihad

In Degel, near Gobir in the northwestern part of present-day Nigeria, Nana Asma'u's father, Shehu Usman dan Fodiyo, preached Islam beginning in 1774–75. He was a prolific author, writing books on the principles by which good Muslims should live their lives. Rural people were drawn to the Shehu, seeking to know from him more about the religion that promised equity and peace. The Shehu, from boyhood immersed in the *Sunna*, viewed his writings as important instructive aids for promoting devotion to its principles of right living. He intended to change society by focusing people away from non-Islamic practices, and toward the spread of justice that was to result from devotion to Islam.

The successive Hausa Kings of Gobir were Muslims whose irreverent habits were not hidden from public gaze. The Shehu had dealings with four of them, starting with the famous warrior Bawa

Jan Gwarzo. It was, however, first Nafata, then Yunfa, who saw increasing interest in the Shehu's teachings as a personal threat to their own royal authority, especially as the Shehu criticized any impious, inequitable traditions that persisted alongside professions of devotion by royalty. These traditions included suggestive public dancing and the accompanying playing of drums and fiddles, and the practice of taking part in ceremonies which were part of the old pre-Islamic religion. Thus the Shehu and his devout philosophy stood in conflict with the Hausa Kings of Gobir for many years. Eventually, the gulf between the Shehu and Yunfa led to a rift, and when his followers were harassed and had their lives threatened, the Shehu decided to depart from Gobir and take his Community with him. He made his escape (*hijra*) from Degel and journeyed to a remote region west of a tract of untilled wasteland where he hoped he and his family and followers would be safe. This set the foundation for the jihad; by removing himself from the king's territory, the Shehu had declared his independence.

> The Shehu tried to meet people in the places where they lived and he explained the tenets of Islam to them in their own languages, imploring them to be of good behavior, to desist from bad practices and pursue the good cause in accordance with the S*unna*. Multitudes of people embraced his teachings and many supported him and his cause so that he became a famous and renowned leader. He moved from place to place through many lands along with his followers to establish the faith, and succeeded in converting the ignorant from the evils of heathen practices to Islam. Through persuasion he succeeded in bringing to his side the learned *malams* [teachers] of his day who were [had been] his opponents. He avoided any form of confrontation with the *sarakuna* [royalty]. Numerous people including many from the royal palaces voluntarily left their homes with all their belongings and joined the Shehu's congregation. These developments obviously infuriated the authorities and led to the subsequent happenings in these lands. (*Tanbih al ikhwan*)[4]

The ensuing conflict became known as the Sokoto jihad, in which the Faithful sought to promote a proper Muslim way of life, and the right of all to follow it. The Shehu's intentions were aimed at offering guidance to everyone regardless of status. He conducted a jihad against those who mixed Islam with customs rooted in the un-Islamic practices of the past. The campaigns waged by different field commanders within a huge geographical area were fought over a considerable period of time. Phase one ended with the defeat of the people of Gobir and the razing of their capital, Alkalawa. Phase two began with the death of the Shehu and the attempts made by the Hausa kings to regain their capital cities. During this phase, sporadic fighting occurred in most places until the end of the nineteenth century. The jihad led to a complete change of government. Hausaland, from being a cluster of unitary states, was amalgamated into a Caliphate. Policy-making was centralized in Sokoto, a new city which had not existed at the outbreak of the jihad.

Nana Asma'u grew up in the midst of these conflicts, seeing her father stand his ground, devoted to Islam and the *Sunna*. Her faith was the foundation of her pursuit of knowledge. Asma'u's efforts to promote reconciliation, education, and justice helped change forever the Muslim culture in which she lived. This was her personal jihad and it took three aspects. First was the preservation and propagation of all that the Shehu stood for. She was indomitable in her defense of his name. Second was the education of women, who were the primary mentors of future generations. She was acutely aware that if captured Gobir women practiced their old customs and passed them on to their children, the seeds of disintegration would be sown. Her aim was to prevent this from happening. Third, she devoted her life to reconciliation and peaceful coexistence, using her wit, her imagination, and her immense prestige to find pragmatic solutions to the problems that faced her.

The Birth of a Daughter, Islamic Education, the *Sunna*, and Sufism

Genealogical charts of Asma'u's Fulani family indicate that they had been Muslim religious scholars for at least ten generations. (See genealogical chart.) Responsibility for the material welfare of this scholarly clan often was undertaken by their pastoralist clansmen, in exchange for scholarly and religious guidance.[5] As Sufis of the Qadiriyya order, material comfort was not among their primary concerns. At the time of Asma'u's birth, her father, Shehu Usman ɗan Fodiyo,[6] who was to lead the watershed Sokoto jihad, was deeply involved in Sufi mystic contemplation during the extended prayer retreats that were part of their community.

Asma'u was born to the Shehu's wife Maimuna and was one of forty children born to his wives and sole concubine.[7] In Asma'u's community the naming of children was the father's responsibility, and her name marked her as noteworthy from birth. Asma'u was a twin, and according to custom, twins were named after the Prophet Muhammad's twins, Hassan and Hussein. Asma'u's twin brother was duly named Hassan, but instead of the name Husseina, the Shehu chose "Asma'u" for his daughter, a name that recalls the extraordinary seventh-century Asma bint Abubakar, daughter of one of the early Muslims. The historical Asma became famous for unhesitatingly aiding her father and the Prophet Muhammad when they were being hunted by their enemies by taking food to them while they were in hiding. For Arabic speakers the name "Asma" resonates at another level: in addition to reminding Muslims of Asma and her deeds, it also means "beautiful" or "noteworthy." The honorific "Nana" serves to deepen her respectability. Thus, Nana Asma'u's name brings to mind a well-respected Muslim woman imbued with positive, heroic qualities.

It may be that Asma'u's father envisioned in his mystical encounters an unusual role for his daughter in the unfolding of the jihad; his choice of her name may reflect that expectation. The Shehu was a reflective man who selected his children's names with care. The fact that he broke with usual practice and did not name his twin daughter according to custom is a strong indication that he believed she was destined to make important contributions. The name he gave her defined her role: like the helper of the Prophet, Asma'u of the Fodiyo clan was destined to foster the spread of Islam.

A classical Islamic education shaped Asma'u's view of the world. This was not simply rote memorization of the Qur'an—although this approach is one by which children first assimilate the word of God—but it involved a rigorous program of study beyond the initial phase. Tutored by her family, Asma'u studied Islamic philosophical texts on prayer, mysticism, legal matters, *fiqh* (which regulates religious conduct), and *tawhid* (dogma). Since the estab-

Ten generations of Nana Asma'u's scholarly ancestors

Muhammadu Fodiyo
m. Hauwa
d. at Degel

|

Shehu Usman dan Fodiyo
m. Hauwa   b. 1754 d. 1817   m. Maimuna
d. 1840s (?)   d. circa 1798

| |

son, Muhammad Bello,   daughter, Asma'u, d. 1864
Caliph 1817–1837   m. Gidado dan Laima, Waziri, d. 1849

| |

His descendants have included most of the 19th-century caliphs and 20th-century sultans, including present Sultan Muhammad Maccido.   Their descendants have included all the 19th- and 20th-century Waziris including the present Waziri, Usman.

Figure 1.2. Genealogical chart

lishment of Islam in the seventh century, Muslim institutions of higher learning have ushered students through a formal course of learning that begins with children as young as four, and continues through the graduate level of university education.[8] Islam was the foundation of Asma'u's experience, and that of her family and peers. Islamic belief presumes that the pursuit of education is not optional, but necessary and central to increased spirituality: knowledge of God can only come through increased knowledge of God's creations as well as through personal experience.[9] Among the Fulani clan known as the Toronkawa, which lived on the western fringes of the Kingdom of Gobir, the Shehu, his brother Abdullahi, son Bello, and daughter Asma'u became religious scholars of the highest order, writing philosophical treatises and preaching the urgency of following the straight path of positive life, the *Sunna.* Asma'u grew up in a household of learned, devout individuals whose profession was scholarship.

Although the Toronkawa clan lived in a rural setting, their faith fostered rigorous home-schooling based on Islamic texts and treatises that had a revered place in the household. The Shehu had a library of hundreds of volumes, all of which were handwritten and stored very carefully in traditional goatskin satchels. It is not known exactly how many books were in his possession, but some indication may be drawn from the fact that in one book alone that he composed, he cited 102 authorities. His own corpus of works ran into hundreds of poems, tracts, treatises, and weighty volumes, all written either in Arabic or Fulfulde on a range of topics to do with Sufism, the law, the *Sunna,* prayer procedures, the conduct of the jihad, political structures, and the education of women.[10] These books were valued properties, transported to safety by camel and horseback when jihad battles forced the community to flee. Whatever else was jettisoned in the bleak days of itinerancy, books were not sacrificed. Nana Asma'u shared the Shehu's aim in teaching, which was to transmit the knowledge of God and help adherents learn how to learn about God themselves. Self-aggrandizement and wealth accumulation were condemned, and students were exhorted to live austere and simple lives. The written works and the tradition of education of the masses that were generated by the Shehu were aimed at the promotion of Islamic practices that followed the *Sunna* of the Prophet Muhammad, the straight path of right living. Both formal and informal teaching were derived from the *Sunna.* The Prophet's exemplary life was taught and imitated.

At the same time, the practicalities of daily life were not to be ignored. The Shehu is said to have made rope, his brother Abdullahi bound arrowheads to their shafts, his son Bello tended his own garden, and his daughter Asma'u inevitably participated in the operation of the domestic sphere. The *Sunna* required respect for the humble tasks necessary to daily life and the avoidance of materialistic attitudes. The Shehu himself wrote: "In his own house the Prophet repaired sandals, sewed [by] himself, gave fodder to his camel used for carrying water, swept the house, ate with the servant and kneaded dough with him, and carried his [own] goods from the market, a job which he allowed nobody else to do for him" (*On the Obligation of Migrating* [*Bayan wujub al-hijira*], 1806: 152). The Shehu's son Bello, quoting a well-known *hadith* about the Prophet, recounted:

> The Prophet Muhammad said, "Allah wants his servants to have means of getting a living. The Prophet Jesus said he met with a man and asked him what he did for a living. The man replied that piety was his profession. Whereupon Jesus said, 'And who feeds you?' The man replied, 'My brother.' Whereupon Jesus said, 'Your brother is more pious than you are.'" (Cited in "The Ethical Foundations of the Sokoto Caliphate" [Doi, 1985].)

Scholarship in a community founded on the ethos reflected in this story would have to speak to practical, not esoteric matters. The nineteenth-century Fodiyo household in which Asma'u grew up was founded on spiritual piety pursued through intellectual endeavors that were in turn grounded in the concerns of daily living. Asma'u was as comfortable in intellectual debate as she was in domestic endeavors, understanding both to be of equal importance to life in this world. The many books written by leaders of the Caliphate—Asma'u's father, uncle, brother, and husband—along with Asma'u's poetic works, were meant as practical guides to individuals at every possible level of social status and degree of academic achievement, from the illiterate to the scholarly. Those who could not read them could hear them; those who could not listen to Arabic or Fulfulde heard Hausa paraphrases, or particular messages in Hausa. Asma'u, like her colleagues, wrote for the betterment of the community and promotion of the *Sunna*, not for personal fame or gain. Authorship was not owned by the individual, nor was personal credit expected for such authorship. What was produced in a literary vein was meant for the spiritual nourishment of the community and was deemed equal in importance to the production of grain in the fields.

Sufism does not require a particular physical setting, nor is it about a teacher's gaining a cult following of students, although the guidance of a teacher is certainly necessary. A teacher's aim in Sufism is to guide students toward union with Divine Truth, in whatever life circumstances they may encounter. Asma'u's education system had no buildings and granted no degrees. It was uniquely suited to the practical needs of a community dedicated to the *Sunna*. The first ten years of Asma'u's life were devoted to scholarly study and were relatively stable, but when she was eleven her community emigrated to escape persecution, and the jihad battles began. There followed a decade of itinerancy and warfare, through which Asma'u continued her studies, married, bore children, and wrote poetic works. In 1807, at age fourteen, Asma'u married Gidado dan Laima, later chief adviser (*waziri*) of the Sokoto Caliphate. At the age of about twenty (1813), she had the first of her six sons. He died as an infant while she was away visiting her father. In 1820, three years after the Shehu's death, as the jihad raged, Asma'u, with two small children to attend to, wrote her first long work, *The Way of the Pious,* a book about morality. She also collated her father's manuscripts and became part of the team which had already set about organizing a new Muslim community in the Caliphate. Throughout this time of active warfare, and in the following period of rebuilding the community, Asma'u was deeply involved in her education and composition, domestic life, and community activism. For the next forty-five years Asma'u continued to write poetic and prose works that dealt with the war, the *Sunna,* and women's roles in the Qadiriyya community.

The Sokoto jihad created social upheaval, leaving among its victims non-Muslim men, women, and children who needed to be assimilated into the Sufi Muslim community. To help accomplish this, Asma'u assisted where appropriate, working within a system of social welfare, according to moral action advocated in Islam. It is likely that she began this work organizing women teachers while in her early thirties; her role as acknowledged leader of women in the community was well established by the time she was forty, when she was known as *"Uwar Gari"* (Mother of All). Recognizing a need for in-home teaching of women in the rural areas, Asma'u trained women students, some of whom, like Asma'u, were free to travel by virtue of their maturity (past childbearing years) and piety. Others were young girls not yet married. These women and girls, known as *'yan-taru* (women disciples), were led by women teachers appointed by Asma'u. Together they disseminated their acquired knowledge among their less-educated sisters in their neighborhoods. Their lessons ranged from instruction in the chapters of the Qur'an, prescribed prayers, and accounts of Sufi women in history, to reports of battle victories, elegies for pious individuals, and a biography of the Prophet Muhammad. They also were tutored in how to pray. Verse poems composed by Asma'u were mnemonic devices for the "lessons" that conveyed this material, as well as the instruments of literacy training; following memorization of the works, students learned to write them and read what they had copied. They then traveled home and shared what they had learned with isolated rural women, who were in this way able to receive an education without leaving their homes. They also were prepared to pass their knowledge on to their children, both boys and girls. In this way, the community's women were educated at a wide range of levels, from loftier, esoteric concerns to basic instruction in issues like daily prayer times, modes of dress, and how to trade honestly when selling the thread they had spun, each according to her needs.

In the Caliphate all teaching had as its foundation the aim of establishing a religious community in which prayerfulness was integral to the smallest of quotidian endeavors. Daily life was imbued with Islamic devotion. Living as a Muslim meant that every moment of one's life was to demonstrate the literal meaning of the term "Islam": submission to the will of God. The population ravaged by the jihad had great need of the potential healing effect of this perspective. Asma'u's role as a teacher in a society torn apart by warfare was to unify diverse peoples through a religious philosophy that emphasized in its precepts the obligation to practice generous social welfare as well as to educate every soul, regardless of gender or social position. Thus, Asma'u's teaching sent ripples of knowledge throughout society. The messages it carried promised the perpetuation of education and mutual aid, aimed at reaching the goal of attaining a higher knowledge of God. Conversely, striving toward knowledge of God was the path toward all things positive in society: education, mutual aid, prosperity, and peace.

Asma'u's Work

Nana Asma'u was educated at home by scholarly women as well as by her father. She was fluent in Fulfulde, Hausa, Tamachek, and Arabic, and she committed the Qur'an to memory. Asma'u educated women at all levels and cooperated with Caliph Muhammad Bello, her brother, in literary ventures which included translating, adapting, and versifying a work on Sufi women. When Bello died in 1837, she and Gidado, her husband, composed nine works which have formed the biographical basis of all subsequent works on the jihad. After her husband's death in 1849, Asma'u played a key role in sustaining the sense of purpose for which her father and brother had become famous throughout the western Sudanic region.

Nana Asma'u wrote nineteen elegies which gave insight into the workings of the Muslim community. She also composed didactic works for her students in whatever language suited her intended audience: Hausa, Fulfulde, or Arabic. In a series of innovative moves she drew rural women into an education network which has survived to this day and, through her poetry, seized every opportunity to draw the attention of the Caliphate leaders to their responsibilities. Her scholarship and piety were as esteemed then as they are now by the scholarly Muslim clerics of her intellectual community, which extends far beyond Sokoto. She is also revered by the descendants of the women she educated and befriended. Nana Asma'u died in 1864 and was buried close to her father in Sokoto. Her descendants have included many famous scholars and the house she lived in with her husband, Gidado, is known as *Gidan Karatu,* meaning it is the home of a family where scholarship is at the center of things, as it was, in fact, in Asma'u's day.

Asma'u was accepted by the leaders of her society both within the Sokoto Caliphate and beyond because of her active engagement in the constructive development of her community, without attention to her gender. Even though the Shehu and the Caliph were Asma'u's father and brother, and her uncle and husband were close military advisers, Asma'u's renown spread as far as Mauritania, as shown by the reverential letters scholars wrote letters to her (see Boyd and Mack 1997: 282–283). It is clear that not only was she privileged in the Sokoto community by virtue of her blood ties, but she was revered there and beyond because of her spirituality, intellect, and literary capability. Her life was at once atypical and one that could readily be understood as a model for those less educated, less revered. A central figure in her community, Asma'u offered guidance that was valued, welcomed, and esteemed by a wide range of individuals. Nana Asma'u's life defied stereotypes, but it was not an anomaly. In her time it was necessary and appropriate for her to be a Muslim woman who was not subordinated, a scholar without a university, and a Sufi who did not retreat from the world. Her life demonstrated the practical side of Qadiriyya Sufi devotion responsive to the immediate needs of a period of turmoil. Nana Asma'u's role as a mentor to others shows that she cannot be dismissed as an exception in her time; she was a woman to be emulated.

Qadiriyya Sufism: The Qur'an and the *Sunna*

Two Nana Asma'u grew up in a Sufi Muslim community. Sufism, often described as Muslim mysti-
cism, is perhaps the most elemental form of Muslim worship, focusing on the spiritual and eschewing the material, corporeal world.
It prescribes a way of life that is simple in all respects, rejecting
preoccupations, like dancing and drumming in social settings, that
interfere with meditation on God and the word of God as conveyed in the Qur'an. Shehu Usman dan Fodiyo sought to model his
own life on that of the Prophet Muhammad, a Muslim practice
called *Sunna,* the straight path (to God).

Asma'u's understanding of Sufism is clearly explained in the
book by her father, the Shehu, *The Sciences of Behavior* (*Kitab ulum
al-mu'amala*), which defines Sufism in the context of religion (in
Arabic, *din*). This book discusses three fundamental aspects of
Islam: jurisprudence (Arabic, *fiqh*), the doctrine of the Oneness of
God (Arabic, *tawhid*), and Sufism. Whereas *fiqh* is concerned with
the outward aspects of Islam, and *tawhid* is about beliefs, Sufism is
about the inward aspects, about the heart. *Fiqh* tells worshipers
what to eat, what constitutes "dirt," how to make oneself ritually
clean enough to address God in prayer, what to do if there is no
water with which to wash, how to pray, how to fast, the obligations
of paying tax (Arabic, *zakat*), and the rules about the pilgrimage to
Mecca *(hajj).* Other features of *fiqh* not found in *Sciences* but ap-
pearing elsewhere in the Shehu's works include the slaughtering of
animals, the making of oaths, marriage, and trade. *Tawhid* encompasses the tenets of Faith: God exists and is omnipotent and om-
niscient; He can accomplish anything He wishes; He has faithful
and trusted messengers; He exists forever and is self-subsistent. No

one can call himself or herself a Muslim who does not believe these things. Sufism, however, is about the qualities of the heart: some lead to damnation and some to salvation. In *Sciences* the Shehu listed those leading to damnation as conceit, envy, vanity, showing off, greed for status, greed for wealth, and boasting. Positive qualities, with which all Muslims are bound to adorn themselves, include repentance, patience, scrupulousness in every aspect, reliance on God, and acquiescence to the destiny ordained by God. The Shehu advises that "every responsible person must learn enough of the science of Sufism to enable him to acquire praiseworthy qualities and to keep him from blameworthy qualities" (p. 33).

The language of the book is direct and not difficult to understand. For example, in speaking of envy, the Shehu comments that it is harmful because it shows anger about what God has decreed, and hatred for the blessing that He has given to someone else: "You are always full of grief and sorrow since God does not cease to pour out blessings on your adversaries. Therefore you are constantly being punished by every blessing [of theirs] you see . . ." (p. 44). "Fear and hope," says the Shehu, "are among the praiseworthy qualities which you must acquire. Fear is achieved by remembering past faults, the severity of God's punishment, your own weakness and the power of God over you. Hope is the joy of the heart when it recognizes the overflowing favor of God and the vastness of His Mercy" (p. 51). The exemplary behavior advocated in this work emulates that of the Prophet and echoes advice given in the Qur'an.

Nana Asma'u acquired from her father respect for the careful balance between the realities of building an Islamic state and living a blameless life. The fascination of the Shehu's personality is that it combined the fundamental characteristics of the Sufi (i.e., one who claims to be in direct communication with God and the Prophet) with those of the lawyer-theologian who derives his knowledge from his understanding of Islamic law (the *shari'a*). Nana Asma'u's nature exhibited a similar balance of these characteristics. The Shehu is one of the few examples of a Sufi also being the leader of a jihad: "It was the Sufi aspect of his personality that contributed to his popularity and the reverence in which he was held. His learning and preaching activities were coupled with piety and self denial."[1] The Fodiyo community in Degel practiced Sufism through adherence to the dual guides of the *Sunna* and the word of God as

Figure 2.1. A house in Goronyo

manifested in the Qur'an. This community sought a closer relationship with God. They observed religious law and sought further spiritual enlightenment by acquiring praiseworthy character and purifying their hearts against conceit, anger, and envy.

The Shehu knew that for ordinary people these matters were not easy. In his book *The Roots of Religion* (*Usul ad din*) he spoke of "the difficulty the common people have in understanding proofs." His son Muhammad Bello described how "he never grew tired of explaining and never became impatient if anyone failed to understand. To all alike he spoke of the things which would be useful to them. And even then, as sometimes happened, he was asked questions in the middle of his talk, he would stop and give an answer."[2] It follows, therefore, that the Qadiri way as led by the Shehu was simple and easy to comprehend. It was a method for the guidance of individuals rather than a whole system of rites; nevertheless, the brotherhood helped to maintain and reinforce the identity of its membership. The Shehu and other Sufi leaders with reputations of devotion, piety, and wisdom sought out upright, "good" men and invited them to join the Qadiri Sufi order. It was done on a personal basis and no initiation rites were involved, just a handshake which was followed by a pronouncement that after every prayer, additional prayers (*zikkiri*) would be said mentioning the name of the founder of the order (Shaikh Abdulkadir). These prayers could be said in private. The importance of *zikkiri* (Arabic, *dhikr*) is evident among scholars of Sufism elsewhere in the region:

> The most important ritual in the *tariqa*s [brotherhoods], however, was, and still is, the *dhikr*. The original meaning of the term, as it appears in the Qur'an, is "remembrance" (of God). In the *tariqa*s, however, the term has acquired a specialised meaning, namely the repetition of God's names and attributes in a variety of special ways. (Karrar 1992: 155)

The Qadiriyya in the Sudan and throughout the Muslim world was a diffused order; its various branches did not share a devotional life. *Zikkiri*, however, was central to Qadiriyya practice in Asma'u's community, and is described and recommended throughout Asma'u's poetic works. Neither the initiation nor the saying of the prayers was complicated, but it was clearly understood that fellow members of the brotherhood had to be respected and its leaders obeyed.

The Shehu told his congregations that he *required* their love, respect, and obedience. He told them that they must love and respect him because without love and respect they would not accept him. They must accept all that he said as true and accept with faith his words.[3] Faith in a master is a hallmark of adherence to a Sufi order. If the Shehu had been an arrogant man, he would not have succeeded as he did. However, all contemporary accounts emphasize his grace and gentleness. It is important to understand that his adherents were ordinary people, not the courtiers of the chiefs. Asma'u's husband Gidado, in underlining the point, said that Allah helped him by ensuring that his followers were all common people, like those who followed the Prophet, and he, like the Prophet, "had sympathy with the common man."[4]

The ease with which people could join the Qadiri brotherhood and the lack of complicated ceremonials must not, however, lead one to conclude that advancement on the spiritual "way" to God

was less than arduous, demanding a degree of self-discipline, prayer, fasting, and asceticism far beyond the capacity of most affiliates.
Sufi masters like the Shehu entered a world of metaphysics which
ordinary language fails to penetrate. It is reported that the Shehu
manifested actions which violated the laws of physics, and that his
contemporary, Sidi al-Mukhtar al-Kunti, flew through the air and
understood the "speech of solids."[5] The vast majority of the Qadiri,
however, carried on with their normal lives of farming and herding,
smithing and other crafts, as before.

The Fodiyo Clan: Qadiriyya Sufis

As Sufis of the Qadiriyya order, Asma'u and her family were
Sunni Muslims who followed the precepts of the brotherhood's
founder, Abdulqadir Jelani (d. 1166) of Baghdad, a saint who is
widely revered.[6] At what juncture in time the ancestors of the
Shehu became members of the order is unknown, but it may have
been an event which coincided with their decision to leave their
home in Futa Toro, near the Atlantic Ocean in what is now Senegal,
and migrate eastward, a migration which, over several centuries,
led them to what is today northern Nigeria in the vast region
known as the western Sudan.

The Fodiyo clan was not alone in its affiliation to what is
known as "the Qadiriyya." Sufism spread in north and northwest
Africa along trade routes and by the fifteenth and early sixteenth
centuries was widespread across the desert fringes, but localized
and based on lineage. There were pockets of Qadiriyya here and
there, each headed by a holy leader who was both a teacher and
a mediator. Son followed father, and daughter followed mother. Abdulqadir Jelani's aunt, Omm Muhammad, and his mother,
Omm al-Khayre, were women of spiritual significance, and it
seems that the education of women was a prominent feature of
Qadiriyya communities. The most prominent *shaikhs* of the order
were sometimes written about in the context of the learned women
who were close to them. For example, Sidi Ahmed al-Bakka'i of
Mauritania (d. 1552) came from a Qadiri community where seventy young girls knew the book called *Mudawwana*[7] by heart, and
the famous Sufi master Sidi al-Mukhtar (d. 1811) acknowledged
the great gifts of his wife, Aisha.

For reasons not completely clear, changes in the international perception and practice of Sufism came in the eighteenth century. In Southeast Asia, India, North Africa, and the Sudan, a new Sufi organization that emerged in about 1750 marked a significant break with the past. What caused the renaissance is controversial but what is undeniable is that the refashioned Sufism involved a shift toward an active public educational approach which meant interaction with local communities. There was also more aware-ness of the universal community of Muslims. This is very impor-tant to Nana Asma'u's perspective on Islam because it means that the work of the Shehu's family was never a localized phenomenon. They were always conscious of who they were, what they were doing, and the validity of their activity in relation to the wider Muslim world. Considering that Abdulqadir Jelani was viewed as a "reviver of religion" (Schimmel 1975: 247), it is significant that he is the patron saint of the Fodiyo community, focused as it was on religious reform. In the western Sudanic region, the Shehu Usman ɗan Fodiyo (b. 1754) led a movement of Sufi Qadiri revivalism which was apparently part of a bigger surge of activity which is as yet incompletely understood.

Although the area is immense and takes years to traverse on camel, scholars in the wider region knew of each other. They com-municated regularly by sending messages and poetry with com-mercial caravans.[8] The scholarly clan known as the Toronkawa, living in what is today northern Nigeria, was part of the main-stream of Islam, and was linked to other Sufis in the sub-Saharan region. Intellectualism was a cornerstone of the widespread Qa-diriyya Sufi community, resulting in prodigious literary output and active teaching as the primary means of spreading the word of God. The word of God was the path to spirituality, and literacy hastened the journey.

Literary Productivity as a Way of Life

In the late eighteenth and early nineteenth centuries, within the sub-Saharan Qadiriyya community there was an intensification of literary production: poetry, treatises, rhetoric, prayer, and praise of the Prophet were newly popular modes of communication for the spread of Sufism. In the course of this period, the literary production of sub-Saharan Sufi groups had far outpaced that of previous centuries.[9] The Fodiyo clan was in large part responsible for the formidable literary output of that period. The overall aim of this activity was the elevation of Islamic consciousness throughout society, regardless of the general level of literacy. In addition to composing formal, scholarly writings in Arabic, members of the Fodiyo clan were aware of the importance of making their works accessible to the average citizen. The Shehu wrote in Arabic, and his works for local consumption were in the vernacular Fulfulde. Others in the family wrote in these languages as well as in Hausa, the language of the majority and the least literate group of society.

The very act of writing in praise of a saint is the act of a Sufi. Nana Asma'u's poems include many elegies. These works were not mere descriptions, but should be read as proof of her Sufism. It is known that the people she wrote about were saints because she described them as being with the Shehu in Paradise. According to Sufi authors, "Allah bestows the gift of describing saints on their followers in order that the energy and zeal of the saints will be transmitted to the disciples,"[10] as Asma'u's husband, Waziri Gidado dan Laima, said in one of his books.[11] Yet another scholar confirms that "discipleship of the saints strengthens the piety of those who follow them."[12]

When writing her elegies Asma'u focused on the Sufi qualities which the subjects of her poems had evinced and their piety. Characteristics such as patience and pleasantness are lauded while riches and status are totally ignored. Someone knowing nothing of the period who ventured to read the biographical poem she wrote about her brother might recite it from beginning to end without being aware that he was a great caliph, or had led forty-seven military campaigns, or was in diplomatic correspondence with far-flung regions, or had knowledge of contemporary European incursions into the Orient. Asma'u did not describe Bello's glamour, only the behavior which did him honor (see appendix). This was in marked contrast to indigenous praise song, in which "there is much bombast . . . the singer lists his patron's exceptional prowess and virtues . . . and describes him rhetorically with laudatory personifications and images drawn from what seems to be a conventional repertoire";[13] an example would be "Male elephant lord of the town /Abdulla, like a bull hippopotamus."[14] Some of Asma'u's elegies were written about people forgotten by history; that she focused on human qualities rather than achievements indicates clearly that she valued character, not status. Her uncle Na'Inna, who died in 1854, held no office and is virtually unknown, but she praised him:

> He was cheerful, loved his family to visit him
> Acted likewise with his neighbors.
> He told them many things.
> He did not concern himself with worldly happenings.
> May God forgive his sins. (*Elegy for Na'Inna,* v. 10)

His life encapsulated the ideal, a life full of the virtues any willing person could try to emulate. "It would be better to ignore all worldly endeavors since we have been told it is not our true home" (*Na'Inna,* v. 4). Asma'u also praised Halima, one of her "very kind, good" neighbors, for living a simple and useful life:

> She was a fine woman with lots of common sense;
> She loved children and adults, treating them fittingly with respect.
> She was religious and kept close relationships in good repair,
> Acting always with never ending patience. (*Elegy for Halima,* vv. 11–12)

Asma'u was well aware of those who had journeyed deep into the mysteries of Sufism and in the elegy she wrote about her sister Fadima commented on the way in which Fadima had entered into religious retreats (Arabic, *khalwa*), keeping strict silences during which she would have meditated and fasted. However, as in all her poetry, Asma'u never excluded the beginner, and in her elegies she offered ordinary people as shining exemplars.

Education

The refashioned Sufism of the mid-eighteenth century focused on educating the common people who were not part of the Sufi circle. At this time the Shehu lived at Degel, which could be described as a "state within a state"; this serves to illustrate that the

Shehu's community was politically and religiously independent of the "country" (i.e., the Gobir region) in which it was situated. Moving with the tide of the Sufi renaissance, the Shehu took the Message to the surrounding peoples and began explaining to them about Islam. He educated them and composed verses in Fulfulde to help them remember his teachings. Others wrote similar works in Hausa. This was the first time that religious verse had been written in the vernacular; though some verse may have been composed before the Shehu's time, "there is no evidence that it was ever written down."[15]

This was a new situation. Prior to 1750 the "state within a state" had been tolerated, but when the Shehu moved out into the community at large and preached, the atmosphere began to change. The Sufis challenged everyone, Hausas and Fulani, men and women, rulers and peasants, to examine their day-to-day behavior. They were advised to drop all customs which were incompatible with discipleship of the Prophet Muhammad (*Sunna*) and turn to the Qur'an, which is of central importance to the education process in Islam and therefore is central to the practice of Sufism. Indeed, the Qur'an has been described as "an anchor of timelessness" (Schimmel 1994: 164) that unifies Muslims throughout both space and time. It is impossible to change the God-given text, and to recite the Qur'an is a sacramental act because it is in the Word that God reveals Himself to humanity. Asma'u relied on the Qur'an as the basis of both her teaching and the written works she used in her instruction. In the works of the Fodiyo family, everything is permeated by allusions to or short quotations from the Qur'an.

Asma'u's succinct work *The Qur'an* (see appendix) is a mnemonic device for teaching the names of the 114 chapters (*sura*s) of the Qur'an. Her work is an aid to recitation of the Qur'an, and therefore should not be confused with the Holy Qur'an itself. Anyone even slightly familiar with Islam would understand that no Muslim would attach his or her own authorship to the word of God, so it follows that any work by that name must be an aid to recitation of the Word itself. The practical nature of this approach is evident when one understands the structure of the Qur'an. Its first chapter is an opening prayer, approximately eight lines in length, and easy to memorize. Thereafter, the verses are arranged in reverse order of length, so the second chapter runs to 286 verses of between six and twelve lines each, with the whole divided into forty separate sections. The next chapter is 200 verses, in twenty sections. It is followed by *sura* 4, "The Women," in 176 verses in twenty-four sections. It is obvious that a student new to Qur'anic studies would become too discouraged if the aim of instruction was to begin memorizing the Qur'an without some understanding of the whole.

Asma'u's intention in her deceptively brief poem was to make God's word accessible to the uninitiated by including the name of all 114 Qur'anic chapters in a verse merely thirty couplets long. Scholars who failed to understand the complexity of her design dismissed the work as one of "little literary interest."[16] Every chapter is cited, whether overtly or in code. Knowing this, and having been instructed in its use, the literate, itinerant women teachers Asma'u had trained (*jaji*s) would have been well prepared to unpack the deeper levels of meaning in each verse. As Qur'anic scholars themselves, each would have memorized a major portion of the Qur'an, if not all of it, in the course of their long education. Equipped with their own understanding of the word of God acquired over many years of study, and instruction in the reasons for the structure of this work, the *jaji*s could use this verse in oral transmission, helping students to memorize and discuss it to understand its meanings. The work is versatile. For those who were learning to write, it could be a copying exercise as well as a lesson in the Qur'an. For those who were even more advanced, the work could allow for discussions of verses at successively deeper levels of meaning. It was an efficient lesson plan for students at any level of study.

In the process of integrating newcomers into a Sufi community, there was no better introduction than studying its source. Asma'u wrote the poem *The Qur'an* in the two local languages, Fulfulde and Hausa, making the work accessible to both the Fulfulde brethren and the Hausa who were beginning to be assimilated into the reformed Islamic culture. At the scholarly level, the work was considered so important that Aliyu ibn Abdullahi translated it into Arabic for that audience. Asma'u's work on the Qur'an promotes an understanding of basic theological premises for all audiences, scholarly or illiterate, male or female, Muslim or not yet converted, allowing for both instruction in a rudimentary understanding of messages contained in the Qur'an and sophisticated discussion of theological issues.

Yet the work loses its dimension when removed from its Islamic context. To the uninitiated it seems a flat listing of names of chapters:

> I pray to God the Glorious
> Through the honor of Alhamdu and the *sura* Baḳara
> And Ali Imarana and Nisa'u and Ma'idatu,
> Lan'ami, La'arafi and Lanfali and Bara. (vv. 1–2)

The Qur'an's first nine chapters are cited in the first two verses alone. Until a student understood the messages contained in each verse, it might be similarly flat, except for one feature: offering the opportunity to recite the names of chapters. Since Arabic is the language of revelation, and the names of the chapters are in Arabic, recitation of these chapter names would have offered talismanic qualities, endowing the poem with the potential to bestow blessings (*baraka*) on the one who recited it. Thus, even from the very moment of introduction to the poem, without any modicum of understanding of it, the poem offered benefit to the reciter. At more sophisticated levels of Sufi study, a student would understand this feature as comparable to the recitation of prayer litanies (*wird*) that characterized Sufi practices. Asma'u explains the usefulness of *The Qur'an*—both the verse and the word of God—near the poem's end: "We are enlightened through the Qur'an, we are prepared / Through His blessings; we will be ready" (v. 24). Focusing ever on the final judgment, Asma'u explains that the Qur'an is the guide that is most useful to new converts and lifelong Muslims alike. She advises by implication that one follow the *Sunna,* and asks for blessings on those who do so:

> Forgive my sins and give me
> Repentance and let me follow the *Sunna,* which protects
> me.
> We ask for blessings on his family and Companions
> And the followers of the *Sunna,* and those who thank God.
> (vv. 26, 30)

Following the message of her work and therefore of the Qur'an guides an individual according to the *Sunna*—the right path and prescription for right living.

Sufi Saints and Politics

The concept of sainthood is as integrally bound to that of Sufism as is education. Many scholars have acknowledged that the Shehu was known as a saint. Louis Brenner compares the saintly status of Sidi al-Mukhtar (1729–1811) and the Shehu, indicating that they both derived much of their authority, both religious and political, from their ascribed *walaya,* which is often translated "sainthood," although a more appropriate connotation of the word is "nearness to God." The *wali* is close to God, a friend of God. He represents the ultimate attainment of spiritual quest in the *tariqa* (brotherhood). In Sufi theory, the *wali* receives his elevated status as a gift from God: his piety and religious exercises are only preparations to receive this gift. His visions and *karamat* (wonders or miracles) are not of his own making but occur through or around him by divine agency. In social practice, however, the *wali* is a source not only of *baraka* (blessings), but also of power: the power to bless, to heal, to judge, to foresee, to transform, and also to curse and bring down the punishment of God.[17] "The *karamat* [blessedness] of the saints was viewed as a Divine gift which cannot be attained by personal effort but vouchsafed by Allah to the chosen as He willed."[18] It is very important to an appreciation of the political development of the area affected by the Shehu's movement to understand that *karamat* is the main constituent of the charisma on which the saint's *(wali's)* prestige, influence, and power over the community depends.

> It is this emotional and impassioned relationship between the *wali* [saint] and his followers that shrouds the former in immense mystery.... Sainthood and its manifestations constituted an important and potent force in the lives of not only those who possessed charismatic qualities, but as well those who lived closest to the *wali* and believed in their capabilities. It is yet another indication of the truth of the maxim important in understanding the history and customs of a people that what they believe and what they perceive as reality is often of more importance

than the cynical opinions of outsiders who have not shared in the same experience.[19]

The Shehu was sanctified as a saint in his lifetime. There was no need for Asma'u or her husband Gidado to do this for him. The same applied to Asma'u's brother, Muhammad Bello, who died while still comparatively young and left the Caliphate without a saintly leader for the first time. The "impassioned relationship" which had existed for sixty years or more and kept the Qadiriyya bonded then was broken. The influence and power the Shehu and Bello had wielded over the education campaign, the jihad, and the setting up of the political entity known as the Sokoto Caliphate were gone. The Caliphate could only be kept alive by reminding people of the two men who had received divine gifts from God. Chosen by Him, they did His will and established the Caliphate. To undermine by sloth what they had done, or attack the polity they had created, or disobey the righteous commands of their successors was to oppose what God had ordained.

Asma'u and Gidado wasted no time. Marshaling their resources, they started to make a written memorial to the two saints. First Asma'u wrote two elegies about her brother, one in 1837 full of anguish, and the other in 1838, a character sketch (see appendix). Then in 1839 her husband rounded off the picture with an account of Bello's miracles. He followed this with a book about the Shehu's *karamat* in 1840, at which point his health began to fail and he wrote no more. So it was left to Asma'u to carry the flame and perpetuate the memory of the Shehu and Bello because she knew at both an emotional and an intellectual level that it was through belief in their divine gifts that political cohesion had been attained and sustained in the past. It appears that it was in 1839 that she first introduced into her works the concept that the Shehu was in Paradise with the saint Abdulqadir, founder of the Qadiriyya. This occurs in an elegy for her sister Fadima:

> May her tomb be full of light and may she be carried to
> Paradise
> Where she will be united on the Day of Resurrection
> with the Shehu and Maimuna and Inna
> And all Muslims, in Heaven. I ask in the name of the
> Most Excellent of mortals who was lifted into Heaven

> For the sake of the Excellent One may we see the One-
> Only God,
> may He put us on the Path.
> And may we see Abdulqadir Jelani, and the Shehu and all
> Muslims . . . (*Elegy for My Sister Fadima,* vv. 14–18)

In a work she composed in 1840, she extended the number of saintly companions to include Shaikh Ahmad al Badawi (d. 1199), Shaikh Ahmad al Rifai (d. 1122) and Shaikh Ibrahim Dasuki (d. 1288). Concluding this poem, *Elegy for Buhari,* with a prayer for victory, she wrote:

> May He make ready all Muslims that Islam will crush
> unbelief,
> and the *Sunna* be triumphant.
> For the sake of the Prophet who exceeds all mortals,
> the leader of the saints of God.
> And Badawi, Rufai, and Dasuki. Also Shehu Degel.
> may God be with them. (vv. 24, 26–27)

To the end of her days, Asma'u reiterated the same message, praying constantly that she would "be united in joy with the Shehu and Bello in Heaven" (*Islam, Sokoto, and Wurno,* v. 21) and that victory in battle would be achieved "for the sake of the Prophet who exceeds all mortals / . . . [and] Abdulkadir, the noble, worker of miracles. . . . / Also Ahmadu Badawi, Rufai, Dasuki, and Shehu of Degel . . . / And Muhammad Bello" (*Caliph Aliyu's Victory, I,* vv. 18–21). The consistency of her approach can be seen in her last dated poem. She was seventy-two years old and the Shehu was long dead when she wrote *Dan Yalli:*

> O Muslims, let us repent and be determined to
> Obey the Caliph's commands.
> And he, in turn, will strengthen us and
> Lead us to victory.
> And the blessings of the Shehu of Degel, son of Fodiyo,
> Who is our leader.
> And the miracles of Abdulkadir,
> The famous saint.
> And Ahmadu Badawi and Rufa'i and Dasuki
> The three on whom we rely. (vv. 15–19)

With her passionate involvement in the affairs of the Caliphate, her acute intelligence, and her high degree of learning, Asma'u was clearly aware that she needed to safeguard the integrity of the Caliphate in the aftermath of the jihad. To the end, Asma'u's works confirmed the presence and purpose of the Shehu as a spiritual leader linked intimately and eternally with the saints who defined Sufi Qadiriyya worship of God.

The Caliphate Community

Three Nana Asma'u was a central figure in a nine-teenth-century Muslim community that mod-eled itself on the original Muslim community of seventh-century Medina. She was surrounded by and equal in stature to those who orchestrated the Sokoto Caliphate, a new social order based on orthodox Islam. Her father the Shehu, her uncle Abdullahi, her brother Muhammad Bello, and her husband Gidado made up the core of public leaders who made and carried out policy. They sought and respected Asma'u's opinion on matters relevant to the organization of the community. In addition, Asma'u was the des-ignated leader of women and responsible for the promotion of education among them.

Sokoto was built as the center of jihad operations and grew as the center of the Caliphate, but the prime movers of this caliphate spent their formative years in the remote village of Degel. This is where both the jihad and Asma'u were born. A plan of Degel, drawn by the Shehu's son-in-law, shows the homes of the sixty-seven men who, together with their families, constituted the core community. This group of highly trained Islamic scholars and their scholarly wives and children ran their own affairs according to their beliefs rooted in the Qur'an, *hadith* (traditions about the Prophet) and *ijma'* (consensus of legal opinion). They were Qadiriyya Sufis who sought to live in the world without attachment to it, but who focused equally on mysticism and following the *Sunna,* the ex-ample of the Prophet Muhammad. These men and women were significantly different from those in the surrounding regions. They were neither rural peasants of Hausaland, nomadic Fulani herders, nor power-wielding courtiers of the kings and rich merchant princes. Degel was unique. It was remote, being several days' travel from the nearest walled city, and very rural. Its houses, the outlines of which can still be seen, were built of small stones coated with wattle and daub. The Shehu's house, where his family quarters and his own private rooms are still discernible, also contained the last resting places of his father and possibly of Maimuna, Asma'u's mother. His students met him under the acacia trees outside his home.

The work ethic of Degel required that everyone be productive. The Shehu's brother Abdullahi said: "Whoever sleeps the sleep of the tired has done right, is forgiven and wakes in the morning of God's pleasure" (Kitabun Niyyati fil aimalil dunyawiyyat waddiniyatt, n.d., folio 14). The scholars farmed, kept cattle, and made rope, arrows, and artifacts. Women spun thread, wove mats, decorated calabashes, and prepared food. Visiting scholars brought gifts of a practical nature with them, and distant well-wishers sent donations of leather sacks filled with grain and the wild produce so much in demand, honey when it was in season. Work was prayerful action, and all aspects of life at Degel were governed and regulated by an Islamic ethos. There was no such thing as a secular life.

Every member of the community was expected to pay close attention to the regulations governing each and every thing. Farmers were advised that the effects of farming extended to animals, birds, and insects. A man was expected to know his land, what best to plant there, and the appropriate tools to use. The handwriting of the manuscript copier was to be clear and easily read by all, not only the very educated. Each Arabic letter had to be distinct and all necessary vowels marked so that the result would be of the maximum use to the majority of readers.[1] The use of cheap ink which would rot the paper was prohibited because "it showed disregard for waste and contempt for the work which had been written out, for it might be a rare work and not easily found. What is more the writer should not write with ink which will easily fade."[2] Any animal slaughtered at Degel was quickly executed in the orthodox manner by cutting the two main blood vessels at the neck and windpipe. After the cut was made, the butcher had to wait until the animal was dead before proceeding. The animal had at all times to be treated gently and not to be slaughtered in the view of other animals of the same kind. In daily commerce, men and women were advised to respond to greetings, bless the sneezer, visit the sick, attend funeral gatherings, keep promises, give advice when asked, and to do to others what they wished for themselves.

Asma'u's Role in the Caliphate

Into this small religious community Asma'u, the most illustrious of the Shehu's daughters, was born in 1793. She and her twin brother Hassan were the twenty-second and twenty-third of their father's children. She was brought up in a society where ideas of family life were centered on propriety and fairness, not repression and domination. Husbands and wives were expected to act pleasantly to each other and to enjoy each other's company. Any man who had more than one wife was required to divide his time equally among them and to educate them all. Children were a special responsibility, and it was held that a child could be molded by means of a good upbringing. "Take the example of fire: parents guard their children from the flames; how much more should they guard them from hellfire."[3] This was a community founded on positive principles, with an atmosphere focused on right behavior, but it was not meant to be oppressive. Those who found it to be too parochial a place would have moved on. Scholars and students in the Shehu's circle were volunteers who moved in and out of residence as their circumstances allowed. There were no walls and no compulsion to stay. It was not until 1804, with the establishment of an army at the beginning of the jihad, that a disciplinarian was appointed to keep order among the troops.

At the domestic level, religious doctrine permeated every detail of life. Asma'u learned to eat with her right hand after first invoking God's blessing. She dressed simply and did not nap during the day because this was said to lead to laziness. She was, however, encouraged to play after school to balance serious endeavors with relaxation. She did not sleep on a mattress because that would have made her accustomed to luxury. She was taught to be humble and respectful, patient and quiet, and to avoid asking for unnecessary things. She had to learn to listen and give way to superiors. She had to be obedient, do the correct ablutions before prayer, learn the law, revere wise people, and apply herself to reading the Qur'an. Good acts were praised and rewarded. Misdemeanors of a trivial nature were ignored the first time around, but further offenses met with quiet reprimands. This was her training as a Muslim of a Sufi order.

Domestic tranquility was interrupted by the commencement of the jihad in 1804. By 1808, after hardship and tribulation, the efforts of the Shehu's forces were crowned by the conquest of Alḳalawa. At that juncture, the plan to build a new city was put into effect. As rural scholars, the sixty-seven families of Degel had no firsthand experience of the complexities involved in running a centralized kingdom such as Gobir, which they had just conquered, let alone a Caliphate which encompassed the huge trading metropolis of Kano as well as important far-flung ancient cities like Katsina, Zaria, and Ilorin. And yet, like the historical city of Medina, Sokoto was to grow to support the needs of the incipient orthodox Muslim community. Thus Sokoto represented a new beginning. Asma'u reported that the Shehu had prayed that "God would cause Sokoto to be in this world forever without taint."[4] She herself went to live there in about 1809 as the young bride of Gidado, who was the special aide of her brother, Muhammad Bello. She saw the walled city constructed before her eyes and she was there when the new government (based on the Abbasid models of the ninth century) was formed.

Muhammad Bello, the founder of Sokoto, was twenty-six years old in 1809. Gidado was about ten years older. Together they implemented the plans which had been the subject of so much discussion, and the focus of several important textbooks, including *Light of Judges* (*Diya al-hukkam*) (Abdullahi dan Fodiyo 1806–1807) and *On the Obligation of Migrating* (*Bayan wujub al-hijira*) (Shehu Usman dan Fodiyo 1806). Important positions had already been allocated by the Shehu at the outbreak of hostilities in 1804. These included the offices of military field commander and officer in charge of discipline. More appointments were made in 1809. Some, like treasurer, were awarded to men such as Sule Wodi who had distinguished himself as a man of valor from the outset, while others were given to men who had grown up in the original Degel community. In due course, Muhammad, the son of the Shehu's elder brother Abdullahi, succeeded his father as Emir of Gwandu, and MuDegel, the son of the Shehu's dearest friend and companion, Umaru Alḳamu, was appointed an adviser to Muhammad

Bello. Mu'Degel, by name a product of the old home, had a sister, Aisha, who married Asma'u's brother Bello. This tightly knit, interrelated group of women and men had been trained from childhood to conform to certain religious patterns of behavior, educated in the Islamic sciences and theology by the same teachers, and taught to focus on the world to come, rather than the temptations of contemporary existence.

The Shehu chose Asma'u to be the leader of women. He himself owed much of his own education to women of previous generations. Asma'u was not the first woman to be respected and relied upon. The Shehu's mother and grandmother had been his teachers, and in the immediate family there were women who were known better by laudatory, descriptive titles than by their given names. His aunt was known as Inna Kabo (Mother of Women with Children) and his wife Hauwa was also known by a "mother" title. In her later years, Asma'u became known to the family by the term *Inji*, a word that indicated her status as an authority. She began to assume her leadership duties while still a young woman. Asma'u was mature and accomplished when she was twenty, an age at which it was common for women to be married and to have already undertaken adult responsibilities. By this time Asma'u had been married for six years and had one child. Furthermore, Asma'u had been educated in classic Islamic scholarship since her youth. She was by the age of sixteen literate in three languages, and fluent in a fourth. She held her own in scholarly debate and was recognized as an effective teacher. Together with her brother Muhammad Bello, she acquired a position of responsibility in the incipient Caliphate.

Resocialization of Enslaved Peoples: Jihad Refugees

New times brought new problems. None was as pressing as the rehabilitation and re-education of the huge population of people incorporated into the new caliphate. Like those among whom the Shehu had proselytized in the 1780s and 1790s, many of these people were barely Muslim, and some were not even nominally so. Sokoto had a large population of uprooted, captured people mainly from Gobir and Zamfara. Of these slaves, men were put to work on nearby farms, where they had to work for their captors from daylight to midday. The remainder of the day was left for them to spend as they wished, and they often chose to farm land of their own. At harvest time, each slave got a bundle of different sorts of grain for himself from his captor's harvest, and the grain from his own land was left entirely for his own use. This farming system closely followed the pattern known to the people from Gobir; it was still in operation in 1921 when British colonial officers were making their assessment reports.[5]

Slaves were required for a multiplicity of jobs in building the infrastructure of the Caliphate. Male slaves worked on the construction of walls, mosques, and principal buildings. They moved rock, prepared wattle and daub, hauled wood to make roof beams, fashioned cane fences, and organized the trains of donkeys which brought water from the river up the steep hill to the Kofar Marke gate on the eastern side of the city. Captured women fell into one of several circumstances: they lived as concubines with their masters, were employed as domestic servants, or worked on the farms with their male partners. The integration of these non-Muslim women into the Caliphate presented complexities similar to those faced by the first Muslim community in seventh-century Medina. They were not Muslim, so their Muslim captors were obligated to facilitate their conversion through education, as was the case for any slave captured by Muslims. Their vulnerability also obligated their captors to provide security for them. This need was addressed by designating some concubines as handmaidens to a man's wives. While conjugal partners to the man, they lacked the rights enjoyed by a wife, but were moved from slave to free status upon bearing a child for the master. A concubine was free to leave her master and the children she had borne, but most chose to stay on. A concubine's descendants inherited the free status of their father. Thus, non-Muslim refugee women were integrated into existing families of the Muslim community, protected, provided for, and socialized according to its precepts.

Muhammad Bello's first slave-woman consort was Dije, and he later added others, including Katambale, the wife of the slain chief of Gobir. Like the Prophet Muhammad, the Shehu had a concubine named Mariya, whose son bore the same name as the Prophet's concubine's son, Ibrahim. The children born of concubines were treated like any of his other children. For example, Dije's son,

Aliyu, was made caliph in 1842, and Mariya's daughter, Maryam, was given in marriage to the Emir of Kano, Ibrahim Dabo.

Women's Organizations and Women's Healing

Gobir men and women were used to being governed by a chief and by the chief's sister, the *Inna*. They exercised authority together, a fact which posed no threat to the regime in Sokoto except that the *Inna* was also the leader of an ecstatic religious healing cult known as *bori,* and many of the concubines who came to the Caliphate were cult devotees. *Bori,* by casting out spirits, was believed to relieve the problems of sick women, especially those suffering from psychological disorders. Furthermore, in *bori,* women found themselves linked to a sisterhood, under the command of the *Inna,* which offered them moral and physical support in times of hardship. The *Inna* treated her followers strictly but with compassion. In a work written when she was in her twenties, Asma'u said that *bori* was akin to witchcraft and both were the work of Satan. She warned that Hell would be the punishment of those who indulged in the practice. *Bori* was a custom that the Caliphate sought to change. Asma'u mediated this conflict by writing a treatise that offered alternative solutions to afflicted adherents of *bori.* The work's medical responses to women's concerns were grounded in the Muslim ethos, and aimed to alleviate both worries and particular illnesses afflicting women and babies. As a highly trained Sufi with widely acknowledged powers of blessedness (*baraka*), Asma'u was regarded as a specialist and was well positioned to deal with the challenges that *bori* presented.

Since many of the refugee Gobir women were *bori* adherents, their introduction into the lives of educated Sufis like Asma'u meant that the spiritual and cultural homogeneity of Muslim homes was in danger of being eroded by what Muslims regarded as a satanic cult. Nevertheless, the Muslim community sought to integrate war victims, not isolate them. Gobir women were installed in Muslim homes as domestic servants or concubines, but in their new living situations some suffered both physical and psychological illness as they grappled with the pain of loneliness, disorientation, and personal loss. These circumstances made *bori* more important than ever to these uprooted women, who were in dire need of healing and rejuvenation.

Asma'u's *Medicine of the Prophet* (*Tibb al Nabi*) (see appendix) was written in Arabic, which put it out of reach of the ordinary person. It was meant to be used by scholars in ways deemed appropriate and seemly, because it included holy Qur'anic verses. Of the forty-six Qur'anic *sura*s quoted, five deal directly with women's concerns: safe delivery in childbirth (*sura* 56); the protection of pregnant women (*sura* 69); the weaning of children (*sura* 85); the successful conception of a male child (*sura* 89); and the safety of infants during childbirth and protection from colic in childhood (*sura* 90). The work addresses illnesses which affected men and women alike, including migraine, inflamed eyes, boils, wounds, piles, deafness, dysentery, inflamed liver, toothache, and depression. Worries and anxieties about such things as poverty, the safety of valuables, forthcoming journeys, the tyranny of those in authority, and debt were included, as well as the general need people feel for reassurance when beset by insomnia, fear, or the dread of witchcraft.

Asma'u wrote that her work "was composed in the fortress of my Shaikh, / the one called Bello, my bosom friend, my brother,"[6] by which she meant it was written with his knowledge and consent. It constituted her response to *bori* and exemplified her resolve. Bello himself was the most important writer on medicine in Hausaland and was the author of ten works on different aspects of healing, including treatises on medicinal herbs and minerals, piles, and eye diseases, and his own work on metaphysical medicine (also called *Tibb al Nabi*), which he wrote after the visit of a distinguished Qadiri scholar from Egypt. This convergence of interest was no coincidence; it illustrates the way in which the men and women nurtured at Degel worked together. They did not look on themselves as aristocrats because they had never been kings. Nevertheless, the new system of government established at Sokoto required every person, great or small, to know his or her own place and acknowledge certain duties that were owed to the state.

The Construction of Community

The Caliphate leaders sought a harmony of effort. The Shehu, along with his brother Abdullahi and his son Bello, organized the new Muslim Caliphate according to classical concepts of state developed by the Abbasids ruling the Arab empire from A.D. 750 to

1258. The ruler needed an army (without which he lacked authority), the army had to be paid for through taxation, and taxes were raised by the state. Justice had to prevail, and this was the responsibility of the ruler, who, in order to achieve his objective, had to cultivate harmony. If the citizenry willfully refused to obey rulers and mocked judges, or if rulers acted capriciously and judges took bribes, then there would be anarchy and the Caliphate would collapse. The Shehu and his cohorts wrote books on government that were of crucial importance, but that were never intended to be used by the general public. For public consumption, in 1812, the Shehu wrote a poetic work that contained his message of community organization and explained the rights and responsibilities involved in the new system. Composed in Fulfulde, this work was intended for scholars and Fulani Muslim reformers. Its refrain, "Be sure of God's Truth (*tabbat hakika*)," has a wide range of meanings, from the rudimentary to the highly symbolic. In the context of each verse, and referring to the admonitions each contains, it is a warning, affirming that this is the truth of things, "there is no mistake." A more esoteric interpretation alludes to its message of Divine Truth (*hakika*), which the Sufi leaders knew as the way to God through the *shari'a*, the highway of the law, the narrow path of the mystic. This poem describes the principles of the Caliphate's theocratic community to the layperson, but it can be read at several levels of comprehension.

Twenty years later the message of *Be Sure of God's Truth* needed reinforcement. The Shehu was dead, and most people could not understand his original message because his poem was written in Fulfulde. In 1831, Asma'u translated the Shehu's work into Hausa, the language of the masses, and in so doing, she created a new work of her own, also called *Be Sure of God's Truth* (see appendix). A brilliant piece, it became one of the most famous of all popular works written during the period and it is still recited to this day. It informs people at all social levels of their obligations to uphold certain duties and responsibilities in an Islamic state. It reinforces the message through a repeated end rhyme of *tabbat hakika*, "Be sure of God's Truth," understood to mean Divine Truth, the Ultimate Reality.

For the average person, *Be Sure of God's Truth* addresses modes of behavior that are incumbent upon good Muslims in any circum-

stances, no matter how difficult. It informs people of their obligations to uphold certain duties and responsibilities in an Islamic
state, "in consideration of the Ultimate Reality," as its end rhyme
repeats. Asma'u's concern to reach the average citizen is evident in
the work's content:

> Let everyone consider and reflect;
> I will give you good advice: be respected.
> Let us continue to follow the Path, and escape retribution.
> Listen to my song and repent
>> And so find salvation, *Be sure of God's Truth.*
> Whether a man has high position,
> Whether he is a ruler or a poor man,
> Whether he is powerful and miserly, or powerful and
>> generous,
> Whoever fails to revere the Caliph
>> Will die ignorant, *This is God's Truth.*
> No matter how pious you are,
> Nor how godly and saintly
> Nor how profoundly learned,
> All who refuse to follow the commands of the Caliph
>> Will be without excuse Hereafter, *Be sure of God's Truth.*
> (vv. 3–5)

Asma'u urges the pursuit of Divine Truth through adherence to Caliphate laws, yet she also emphasizes the obligation of the caliphs
who make the laws to set examples as followers of Divine Truth.
Asma'u appeals to the ruled and the rulers alike. Each individual
is expected to consider his or her own position in relation to the
Ultimate Truth that should be every person's focus. The foundation
of the community was of primary importance, and that is clarified
here, for scholars, rulers, and warriors. Verse after verse counsels
patience, justice, fair play, loyalty, righteousness, and forbearance.
Harmony was the political objective, a goal which matched the
harmony of the inner self with God, sought by Sufis.

Asma'u's belief in the redeeming value of education is also
made clear. She urges the pursuit of Divine Truth through education, which path should be open to all, regardless of gender, age,
political level, or socioeconomic status. In this and other works she
emphasizes that once a man or woman embraced Islam, that person became her co-religionist and therefore one of the "brethren"

or "friends." Asma'u did not discriminate between people of different ethnic backgrounds, but instead included them in her community. She urged people to join the community regardless of status, ethnicity, or language. In fact, the poem makes this point in Hausa, the language of the people of Gobir who had been her father's fiercest opponents.[7] Her message was that the path is open, and the ambition to follow it should be every individual's obligation. Asma'u expected every person to pursue the Truth, demonstrate upright behavior, and seek knowledge.

Considering that these works were used in educating women secluded in the home during their childbearing years, it is significant that this work provided a detailed portrait of the varieties of people in society. In that respect, it furnished an image of the public world to which a secluded woman might not otherwise be privy. At the same time that it documented an unfamiliar world, it established for the individual woman her right to consider herself a full member of the collective that made up the Caliphate. In addition, the process of transmission of the work by oral recitation also meant that the act of teaching and learning was a collective process, quite likely reaching many within earshot of the lesson, as the women's voices carried over from one open-air compound to the next. Therefore, the teacher's work involved bringing the wider world into the domestic sphere, without limiting it to that private domain.

The collective character of the Muslim community depended upon each individual's appropriate fulfillment of his or her role. The duties of community are expressed in their broadest form. Asma'u's work focuses specifically on the importance of women as socializers; it compelled teachers to transmit and explain the poetic work, whose message in turn compels students to give of themselves as citizens for the social and spiritual betterment of their society. The education process promoted by Asma'u and her followers shows a deep understanding of community and the work needed to maintain it.

Practical Poems

At a practical level, Asma'u addressed the needs and concerns of the average, uneducated members of society. The *bori* spirit possession cult was a prime means of ministering to the psychological, social, and emotional crises that threatened individuals. Maintained by women, the cult represented a traditional, non-Muslim vehicle for counseling and rehabilitation. On occasions of devastating drought, the cult would act to effect positive change. Rather than simply prohibiting *bori,* Asma'u sought to provide an Islamic substitute. In *A Prayer for Rain,* which was written in Hausa for general consumption, she appeals to *bori* members to turn their energy to prayer rather than spirit possession.

This poem also extended its message to *bori,* not ignoring the possibility of *bori* intervention to promote rainfall, but embracing and displacing it. The message is clear: if you need rain, pray to God for it, not pagan spirits. This news is clearly intended for non-Muslim women, who were the majority of *bori* adherents. Of the undesirable activities cited in this work, *bori* is the one most closely associated with women. In *A Prayer for Rain* Asma'u admonished people to "Repent of using magic, attending *bori,* and gambling / Hellfire will be the reward of those who do not repent" (v. 12). The ubiquity of drumming at non-Islamic *bori* spirit possession rites was clearly intended as a focus of this work, in which Asma'u clarified the acceptable occasions for drumming in the community, none of which were connected with *bori.* The times when drumming was allowed were specified in this work: they were limited to the need to call meetings, for the departure or encampment of an army, for communal labor, or when traveling (vv. 15–17).[8] Asma'u warned, "But do not allow drumming at weddings to accompany wild dancing. / It is sinful: [resulting in] worldliness and forgetfulness" (v. 18). Asma'u stated clearly that one should avoid places "where there is immoral drumming and chatter / For men and women mix together on these occasions" (v. 14). As is typical of Asma'u's other works, *A Prayer for Rain* addressed a timely concern in a straightforward, practical manner. She advised against *bori,* but only while offering an alternative practice to fill an obvious need, and explaining why the old practice was dangerous, and what the average person was to do about it. Caliphate women were to be unified under common principles, even those extending to their manner of dealing with environmental issues such as drought.

A Prayer for Rain reinforced the importance of women's roles in a Sufi community. It is logical that an environmental concern as important as rain should be addressed, but in this work Asma'u brought concern for rain under the rubric of a Muslim Sufi ethos. Rather than ignoring a non-Islamic practice connected to interest in rainfall, she faced it head-on and transformed it into a Muslim's rightful concern, about which it was appropriate to pray, explaining:

> The existence of water is a mercy to the world,
> Like fire and iron whose value is inestimable.
> O Lord, give us a beneficial heavy rainstorm
> For our relief. Your gifts are unending.
> Bring life to our crops and cause them to grow
> Many requests are made on You to exercise Your power.
> In the name of the excellent one, Your Prophet Muhammad,
> We seek aid from You and we will not fail to find it.
> (vv. 5–8)

Asma'u gave new perspective to environmental concerns, drawing the wish for rainfall into her framework of Islamic concerns, not only reminding people to seek aid from God as they followed the *Sunna* (vv. 9–11) but, as is common in all her works after 1838, calling too on the Sufi saints al-Jelani, Rafa'i, Badawi, and Dasuki.

Incentive to Conform

Fear This, the most powerful of her admonitions, which is not dated, is a graphic description of the eternal horrors to be faced by those who do not reform. The poem might have been written at a period of frustration concerning the progress of the community, for its urgency is gripping. Its length is imposing (ninety-nine quintains), and its language is terrifying. It recounts a vast array of eternal torments in Hell, including being fried alive, flogged, blinded, clubbed, starved, frozen, choked, melted, squeezed, and forced to drink disgusting liquids. The aim of this work was to encourage people to prepare for death, the ultimate fate:

> To me has been revealed something terrifying about
>   death.
> I fear God who created me and gave me prosperity.
> The receiver of blessings should thank God, otherwise he
>   will perish.
> I thank the fearful One who controls instruments of fear.
>   Who, when he causes people to die, removes them

without trace, just as a site from which not even palm
seedlings are left.
    God has told us about the conditions attached to
    entry into Heaven ⟶ in Sunna & Qur'an
In books and elsewhere. So listen and remember.
All people, great or small, die.
Their very existence on earth is obliterated.
    Then their graves are rent and all human beings rise
    amid terrible fear. (vv. 1, 15)

As if the simple prospect of death were not enough, Asma'u describes the particular pains to be endured by the unfaithful:

Those who have refused to acknowledge the Truth, the
    pagans, are condemned.
The Angels of Death take them to the Gates of Hell and
    incinerate them.
They are squeezed and pushed in.
They go to the Well of the Fire of Hell where they are
    burned.
    The Fire encircles them, thousands and thousands on
    every side fully enclosed.
They seek to take drafts of water
But are prevented because it is the aim to make them
    thirsty and to sweat.
They are shown distant flowing water,
But their drink is the pus which comes from sores, and
    urine
    And feces mixed with vile, noxious poisons.
A person who has killed a Muslim is seized, beaten, and
    then melted in a pot.
The head of the oppressor is split open.
Those who have done forbidden things are crushed again
    and again.
Thatching needles and charcoal await womanizers, and
    thorny sticks.
    And huge snakes, which are thrust into their clothes.
(vv. 29, 56, 80)

This work was meant to be recited; that it was written in Fulfulde
means that it was intended for an educated audience. It is possible
that it was meant for 'yan-taru teachers' education, allowing them

to convey to their students the perils facing the impious. Clearly, Asma'u assumed that if gentle encouragement was ineffective, terror might spur repentant action.

Over the years, Asma'u's works sought to reshape the community through education. A consummate teacher, Asma'u drew on a wide range of tongues, voices, and tones, sure to find a means of appealing to the greatest possible audience. Her works were aimed at Sufis and *bori* adherents alike, with the same degree of conviction. Using an extensive variety of tones and tactics, she always sought the best means of reaching the audience. All this effort was orchestrated in the promotion of a unified, pious Muslim community.

As the daughter of a man who spent his life trying to change society, Nana Asma'u was imbued with the spiritual ethos that constituted the foundation of the Caliphate community. Her written works reflect that clearly. Her father, the Shehu, like the Prophet Muhammad, whose life was the model he followed, spent years traveling in regions which were for the most part very un-Islamic, provinces like Zamfara and the riverine areas bordering the Niger at Illo. Living conditions while traveling were not comfortable: the Shehu did not frequent the courts of the rulers, but lived in simple accommodation outside the towns. Asma'u was used to his preaching to ordinary people in the places where they congregated, the markets; among his audiences would be pagans, "brazen worshipers of stones and spirits who neither prayed nor fasted nor gave alms and who blasphemed against Almighty Allah." She grew to appreciate his gentle manner, equitable approach to the masses, and immeasurable patience with those who required further explanation. "He preached about the requirements of the *shari'a,* the *Sunna* of the Prophet, about turning people from error to righteousness and the extirpation of devilish innovation."[9]

Much of this may seem as though it was too hard for ordinary people to understand. "Brazen worshipers of stones" would have found it difficult to make a quick leap to an understanding of the *Sunna.* However, a study of the Shehu's very early works in Fulfulde, written in the 1780s, reveals how he spoke in their own languages to the Hausa and the Fulani about the customs they had to drop if they wished in all sincerity to be proper Muslims. He preferred a reasoned and persuasive approach. There were definitely no conversions by the sword. [He spoke openly about men who treated their wives improperly; who failed to provide them with clothing, thus forcing them to seek paid work; men who were unfair in divorce, and unkind when they favored one wife over another. He told the Fulani that their *pulako*, or full-blooded macho behavior, was outdated, and that the *sharo*, the customary trial of pain endured by strong young men, was unacceptable.] He discouraged the custom of refusing to speak the name of a firstborn son or daughter. The Shehu did not favor Hausa customs over Fulani ones, or vice versa, but condemned all in like manner. Furthermore, he spoke to ordinary people about the things they actually knew about from their own experience. For example, he did not talk esoterically about theology but pointed out the uselessness of woodworkers leaving grain as sacrifices to tree spirits and the futility of animal sacrifices at the great rock outcroppings. To refocus their energies, the Shehu recounted the life of the Prophet Muhammad, whose example they could follow as Muslims. Through his example the Shehu gained a large following, and when he had finished a preaching tour, which might have taken months if not years to complete, he returned home to Degel, situated in a part of the country where twelve generations of his ancestors had lived.

Asma'u understood and respected the aim of imitating the life of the Prophet, and sought to follow such an example. She too spoke to people in their own languages. Her works reflected in both content and style a sensitivity for her audiences, and always emphasized the spirit of community that she and her cohorts sought to mold. The community they endeavored to create was modeled on historical precedents of Muslim communities whose philosophical basis was spiritually grounded and ubiquitous. It was evident not only in law and commerce, but in the smallest detail of a person's life. Asma'u explained through her works how to pray, heal, work, and converse, what to eat and when to sleep. All this was couched in the framework of spirituality that aimed to create a community based on the *Sunna*.

The Poetic Tradition

$\mathcal{F}$**our**   In A.D. 610 while meditating in the cave of Hira on a Meccan mountainside, Muhammad began to receive revelation through the intermediacy of Jibril (Gabriel). The first occasion upon which he received it is known to Muslims as "The Night of Majesty."[1] Because he was illiterate, Muhammad was at first unable to perform the "reading" that Jibril commanded with the words "Read! Recite!" Nevertheless, Muhammad soon discovered that divine inspiration led him to recite the words of God. These messages were to become scripture when all Muhammad's revelations were collected in the Qur'an some forty years later, just after his death. Since that time, Islam, which literally means "submission to the will of God," has involved active study of the Qur'an, literally "the recitation." Literacy is so important to Islam that a common expression in Muslim cultures is "The ink of the scholar is more sacred than the blood of the martyr." Indeed, to an extraordinary extent, literacy is the cornerstone of Islam. For Muslims, knowledge of every aspect of life is the means of approaching God. This perspective has fostered scholarship, literacy at all levels, and a long tradition of literary productivity in the Muslim world.

By the time the Shehu died in 1817, Asma'u's accomplishments were well known. At the age of twenty-four, the young scholar was fluent in Arabic, Fulfulde, Hausa, and Tamachek and had intimate familiarity with the works her father had composed as well as the reference library he had accumulated. The loose-leaf manuscript texts were kept in specially made leather covers (*tadarishi*), which in turn were placed inside goatskin bags (*gafaka*). They were the most important of all their possessions and were treated with respect, but in time their pages suffered the attrition of constant use, exposure to the searing dryness of the semi-desert air, and occasional accidental storm damage. Books, therefore, were constantly being copied, a time-consuming process which demanded of the copyist concentration and a sense of religious purpose. A library the size of the Shehu's did not have rows of books on shelves. It was a place where books were in various stages of renewal, a scriptorium.

After the Shehu's death his heirs decided not to divide the library but to keep it intact.[2] They also agreed to reassemble all the texts and ensure that copies of the tracts, poems, and books that their late father had authored were preserved. The responsibility for doing all this, according to Asma'u, was given to her husband, Gidado, whose tasks as *waziri* (chief executive) of the Caliphate included making long journeys away from home, keeping the mosques and city walls in good repair, having frequent meetings with the caliph (Asma'u's brother Muhammad Bello), and acting as a general when the army went into battle. In other words, Gidado had immense responsibilities, especially in the period just after the Shehu's death when a general insurrection was staged by those the Shehu had defeated, a period which coincided with the reorganization of the great library. Asma'u, with her consummate linguistic skills, was exactly the right person to have played a strategic role in assembling the library. Her piety (she had committed the Qur'an to memory) and her energy (she had recently ridden to Kano and back, a distance of 620 miles), together with the trust her husband and brother had in her, gave her all the authority she needed. In the eyes of some scholars today in Sokoto the reassembling of the library was a re-enactment of the task accomplished by the Prophet Muhammad's successor who compiled written versions of the divine revelations known as the Qur'an.

As a woman Asma'u had access to the interior family part of the Shehu's house and to the rooms of his wives where books were stored. Her mother, Maimuna, had died when she was a child, but the two wives responsible for bringing her up, Aisha and Hauwa, were still living in the Shehu's house, although Hauwa (Muhammad Bello's mother) was given another room because her husband had died in her apartment. It was there that he was buried, his tomb becoming a place of pilgrimage.

Figure 4.1. The entrance to Nana Asma'u's room at Gidan Waziri

The natural course of Asma'u's education was for her to continue reading, writing, and teaching upon her maturity. Because piety and scholarship are integrally connected in Islam, Asma'u's pious family expected that scholarship would be a continuing part of her life. Yet no one in this community pursued scholarship at the expense of daily obligations. As Asma'u married and had children, she did not engage in research in isolation:

At the same time that she was engaged in [cataloguing the Shehu's works], she continued to be responsible for a household of several hundred people, seeing to it that their daily needs for food, clothing, and shelter were met. During this time her husband Gidado, acting as vizier [*waziri*], was often departing for an outlying area on assignment; such journeys would have required special preparations and provisions, for which Asma'u would have been responsible. Furthermore, she would have had to play host to the many travelers who arrived at her home to visit her husband, providing them with all the comforts that were expected. As a figure of authority, Asma'u would also have been responsible for mediating disagreements, a talent which seemed to be a part of her character, and for which she was noted all her life. Her brother Isa commented on her talent for mediation in his elegy for her. Asma'u's scholarship, sufism, and responsibilities were all related to her promotion of sufi values, representing the aims of the community. Her talent for executing her many roles with consummate skill made her one of the central figures of her community. (Boyd and Mack 1997: 8)

Nevertheless, scholarly women were common in Asma'u's clan. Asma'u herself calculated that there were "as many as a hundred" (*Sufi Women*, v. 75) (see appendix). Asma'u's grandmothers and great-grandmothers on both sides of the family were known to have been educated women who focused their studies on the Arabic poetic composition that is the style of the word of God, just as other Muslims had done for centuries before.

The Arabic poetic mode of Islamic literature has been a major form of literary productivity since then. It includes verse forms that are admonitions, biographies of the Prophet, didactic verses, historical chronicling, panegyric, Qur'anic commentary, and Sufi recitation. Many of these styles, while distinct, are very similar; for instance, Qur'anic commentary (*tafsir*) and accounts of the Prophet's life (*hadith*) are prime sources for Islamic education, yet *sira* is the term for accounts of the Prophet's life and accomplishments, while *madih* is the term for works praising the Prophet in both life and death. The *qasida* denotes praise of a patron, or, in a more religious context, a praise eulogy for the Prophet.[3] Such a multiplicity of genres generated a comparably rich and complex system of standard rhyme schemes as well as metric patterns within the lines themselves. Another technique commonly found is the *takhmis*, an Arabic word derived from a verb meaning "to make into five." Thus a five-line verse is created by adding three lines to an existing couplet. A student could honor a poet by making longer verses from the poet's original work in couplets. Also important in Arabic verse form are techniques such as the acrostic and the chronogram. This rich body of Arabic verse genres and forms comprised a major portion of the materials used in Islamic education systems since Islam's inception.

In the course of her education, Asma'u studied works in Arabic Islamic verse. The variety of styles evident in her corpus of works attests to her mastery of sophisticated techniques. Notable among her works discussed here are those that demonstrate ability in the creation of various poetic forms and styles: the acrostic (*So Verily*) (see appendix); the creation of the *takhmis* (*Fear This*); panegyric (*madih*) and end rhyme *(In Praise of Ahmada)* (see appendix); techniques for energizing the standard form (lack of opening doxologies in *Destroy Bawa* and *Dan Yalli*);[4] *manzuma*, the versification of pre-existing prose works, and interweaving of the imagery of classical texts into her own works.

Acrostic Technique

Acrostic poetry has long been a popular style in the literatures of many cultures, although it was rare in the Fodiyo community. In an acrostic the first letter of each line forms its own message, which relates to the message contained in the verses of the whole work. In Asma'u's *So Verily* the message of poem was based on the sentiment in the Qur'anic verse "so verily with every difficulty there is relief" (*fa'inna ma'a al usri yusra*), with the end letters spelling out that Qur'anic line. (See figure 4.2. Note that in Arabic script, the lines read right to left.)

Asma'u's poem can best be understood through the family oral tradition about it. The story goes that, with the enemy massed and advancing on Asma'u's town of Sokoto, her brother Muhammad Bello, chief of the Muslim forces, returned to town to address the people. He also delivered a message to her. His intent was to calm her anxieties on the brink of battle. As the war drums beat outside the town, Asma'u composed a response to Bello's poem, creating it the same length, and responding to his rhetorical questions, such as "Are you apprehensive knowing that your Lord is powerful?" (Bello, v. 6), and "Do you think He would neglect one who is hopeful of Him?" (Bello, v. 14). Asma'u's responses confirm the faith that both needed as a source of fortitude in the face of difficulty. She says, "Anyone who says he requires nothing of God is either ignorant or an unbeliever. / Everyone who seeks God's help will receive it, for God allows people to make requests" (vv. 4–5), concluding logically, "We pray for victory and that the rebellion of [the enemy] may be overcome" (v. 9). The invasion of the Caliphate came to an

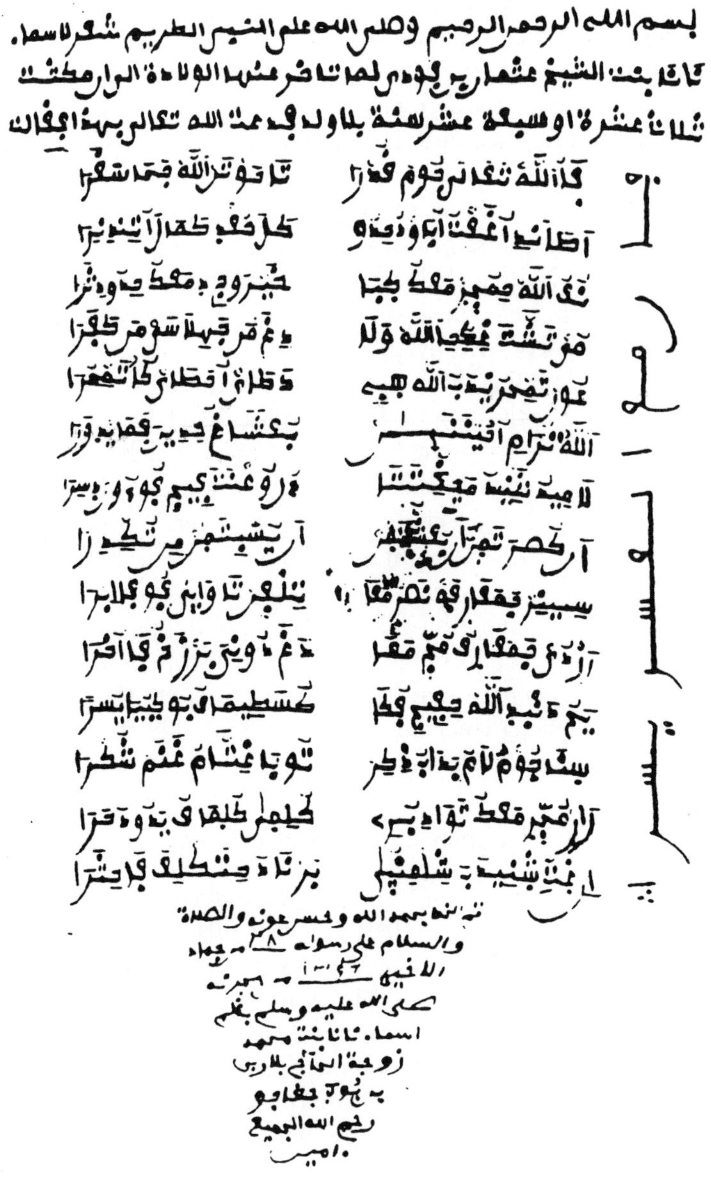

بسم الله الرحمن الرحيم وصلى الله على النبي الكريم شكرا اسما

كان بعث الشيخ عثمان بن فودي لما تناصر منها الولاة الوار مكث

ثلاث عشرة او سبعة عشر سنة بلا ولد فعبد الله تعالى بهذا الفال

تا تو تر الله بحد اشعر	كان الله نفدا تر يوم فذا
كل خلق طعا آلي بذير	اطاعك امفت ابو ذيدو
بيرو بو دمعك يدو ثرا	نق الله يميز عك بجا
دغم قر بيلا سو مر طبرا	مو تشة يكيا الله ولا
د طلاق آطلاق كأ نفعرا	عو تفخر يد بالله بيه
بعنشاع دديو فعذيو قزا	الله ترام آفينفي
ور و عنذ كيم كو وو وسر	لا مية نيبد ميك نسا
آر يشبنمز مر تلد را	آر كصر تمر تا بع فبر
ينلعرتا وابن كو قلابرا	سيبيبز بعقار قه نر قغا را
د غم د وين برز فم قيا اثرا	آرد ك بمقار ك مم مقر
كسطيغا قبو ييبا يسرا	يح د نبج الله يجيع فغا
تو با غنتام غنم شكرا	بستا جوع لا ام بذاح ذطر
كحمم طبعا ق يدو تعرا	آر مبر عك تواديس
بر تا د متكليق قا يترا	ا بمذ نبنيد ب شلغيا

نبنه بحمد الله ونسرعونه والصلة
والسلام على رسوله عليه جماه
الا فيه سنة . . . سيرته
صلى الله عليه وسلم بغم
اسما . كانا نتد محمد
زوجة ابنا في بلاربن
ب جوع بغلا بو
رفم الله البميع
با مين

Figure 4.2. Facsimile of Nana Asma'u's poetry

abrupt conclusion when the leaders of the Gobir-Tuareg army failed to agree about tactics and dispersed in disarray, leaving huge quantities of equipment in the field. Opponent Ibra, in his anxiety to flee the scene, rode his horse so furiously that it collapsed under him.

Bello and Asma'u must have been extremely competent poets to have been able to communicate by writing acrostics for one another. He wrote in Arabic, she in Fulfulde. He took as his text the very well-known verse of reassurance from the Qur'an; she took the same one. Neither Bello nor Asma'u had any time to spare on that day. With the enemy camped outside the city walls, neither was in a tranquil or reflective state of mind. According to tradition, the enemy's thudding drums were clearly heard by the inhabitants of Sokoto, just as the glow of their campfires had been seen during the previous night. The terrifying excitement which made their blood course produced resolution in Bello, apprehension in Asma'u. It also sparked the clever exchange between brother and sister, Caliph and chosen daughter, which is evident in these poems. Their sense of mutual support in the face of danger is unusual and indicative of the strength of their belief in both one another and their cause. How many examples are there in history, or indeed how many acrostic poems of any kind have we found in the poetry of the era? The former chief archivist of the Sokoto History Bureau, Alhaji Bashir, knew of none.

Technique: *Wa'azi* and *Takhmis*

Fear This is a prodigious work intended to educate in the Sufi mode; it recounts the horrors of the afterlife that are the certain fate of unbelievers. Asma'u composed this work by adding lines of *takhmis* to a work composed by Muhammad Tukur, a student of her father's whom she had met at Kirare when she was ten, prior to the first assault on Alkalawa. Muhammad Tukur had in turn modeled his work on the account of the horrors of Hell in the Qur'an.[5] Evidence of this is clear throughout the work. The aim of such a work was twofold: not only did it warn people of the effects of sinfulness, but it also demonstrated the author's familiarity with the Qur'an, and his or her ability to teach it.

Considering its tone, this work may be considered exemplary of admonitory verse, the *wa'azi* or warning style of Arabic poetry.

Muhammad Tukur and the Shehu's brother, Abdullahi ibn Muhammad, were the first in the region to compose *wa'azi;* these verses demonstrate their familiarity with classical Arabic verse (Hiskett 1975: 41) and were effective as learning devices for converts to Islam. To create this work Asma'u employed the common Arabic poetic technique of *takhmis* (in Hausa, *tahimisi*), which involves prefacing an existing couplet with three more lines while maintaining the original rhyme and meter.[6] Such re-creation of an existing work indicates respect for the author of the first version, usually a *shaikh* who intended the work to be recited as a pious exercise. The mark of an effective *takhmis* is the smooth integration of imagery, such that the images in the *takhmis* feed into the two final lines, creating a seamless verse. In the following examples from *Fear This,* the original couplet is in italics, with Asma'u's additions preceding it:

> To me has been revealed something terrifying about death.
> I fear God who created me and gave me prosperity.
> The receiver of blessings should thank God, otherwise he will perish.
> *I thank the Fearful One who controls the instruments of fear,*
> *Who, when He causes people to die, removes them without a trace just like a site from which not even palm seedlings are left.*
> Anyone who has to become involved in World affairs should not act foolishly;
> The best thing is to pay no attention to the World, for it is like a cramped room, so go prepared;
> Yes, the best thing is to divorce the World, which constantly mutates.
> *Fear the World with its endless vacillations and do not take delight in it.*
> *Be fearful by day and by night as the passing days bring death nearer.*
> In what God has instructed let us become engrossed. Do not weary, increase your efforts and sincerely repent.
> Do not revert to former habits.
> It is forbidden to act as though death does not exist: it only strikes once.
> *Fear death's approach, which comes with grief and sickness,*

And pain and agony as fierce as the wind of the hot season.
And also the death rattles and the bursting of blood
vessels:
The way to the grave is accompanied by dreadful thirst,
And the last breath is accompanied by much groaning.
Like whips, swords, and clubs are the throes of death.
Life on that day of departure to the grave may bring one to
pleasures or hardships.
Your grievous sins have all been recorded, and even the less
important ones.
Everything you have done is remembered, even what you
have said.
Everything about you will be seen in the grave.
You will meet up with everything you did in the past. It is
accumulated, and awaits you.
Anyone of worth will be rewarded, and the evil doer will be
punished. (vv. 1, 6–9)

The *takhmis* shown above expands the thought contained in the original couplet. As the description of the pains of Hell become more explicit, so does Asma'u's embellishment. About those who are condemned she writes:

They are made afraid; they shudder because of their evil
deeds.
Shocked and agitated, they do not know where to turn.
Fire has been heaped upon them, their heads split open
and they are scattered.
They go to the Day of Judgment, one by one, fifty thousand of
them,
And they are frightened, parched with thirst and starving:
They are on their way to Hell. (v. 21)

In this verse the original portion alludes to a verse from the Qur'an: "The Companions of the Fire / Will call to the Companions / Of the Garden: 'Pour down / To us water or anything / That God doth provide / For your sustenance.' / They will say: 'Both / These things hath God forbidden / To those who rejected Him'" (VII: 50). Asma'u's *takhmis* provides more detailed imagery for effect. Similarly, the following verse refers to Qur'anic verses: "And when they are cast, / Bound together, into a / Constricted place therein, they /

Will plead for destruction / There and then! / This day plead not / For a single destruction: / Plead for destruction oft-repeated!" (XXV: 13–14):

> Forever they will be in a deep place,
> For all those for whom there is no escape enter deep pits
> They are left there, together in the heat.
> *They are locked together in scorching heat. They seek a*
> *Place to lay their heads, but there is none. They were*
> *told about these torments, but they refused (to listen).*
> (v. 22)

The Qur'anic image of being bound eternally and irrevocably to hellfire is powerful: "As to those who are / Rebellious and wicked, their abode / Will be the Fire: every time / They wish to get away / Therefrom, they will be forced / Thereinto, and it will be said / To them: 'Taste ye / The penalty of the Fire. / The which ye were wont / To reject as false'" (XXXII: 20). Asma'u's verse 30 contains similar imagery:

> They are bound and driven toward the Fires, and are
>   thrown in.
> They are forcibly pushed—
> They want to get out, and they scream
> *When they are brought, and are about to go in, the Fire*
>   *welcomes them with a thousand tortures.*
>   *The tortures are laid out. They engulf the body. Every single*
>   *person is in deepest despair.* (v. 30)

The Qur'an is clear on the horrors to be endured by those who do not believe in God: "Those who reject / Our signs, We shall soon / Cast into the Fire: / As often as their skins / Are roasted through, / We shall change them / For fresh skins. / That they may taste / The penalty: For God / Is exalted in Power, Wise" (IV: 56). This is evident in verses like the following from *Fear This:*

> Many thousands are condemned in a trice.
> The Fire is told to consume them speedily.
> So they are brought to it and it engulfs them head to toe.
>   *The fire splits their skin, bones, flesh and sinews.*
>   *They are butchered until body fluids and blood flow.*

The intestines and internal organs are poisoned and
Thousands upon thousands of people fill the bottom of the
    pit.
For ever they lie in the pit bottom,
    Once in the pit, in a split second seventy thousand are burned.
    They get another skin, and the whole process is repeated
    within the encircling fire. (vv. 35–36)

Fear This is a work with a multiplicity of purposes: admonition, teaching behavior, teaching the Qur'an, and acquiring spiritual benefit through its recitation. Asma'u's *takhmis* enhance the work's efficacy on all these levels. This discussion focuses on the usefulness of the imagery presented in the *takhmis*, concentrating on the work in translation. Much of the structural literary quality of the *takhmis* is lost in translation, but it should be noted that as Asma'u wrote it, the piece follows the original work's form, true to its metric and rhyme schemes, both of which disappear in translation.

End Rhyme

The wonderful gifts of talent, expressive language, and great knowledge represented Asma'u's power, for they enabled her to address and satisfy the needs of all her students, beginners as well as *shaikh*s, simultaneously. Her multilayered poetry delighted diligent students because she led them to explore aspects of Arabic classical verse at an intellectual level, while never failing to address the needs of the beginner.

Consider the poem *In Praise of Ahmada,* a work of fifty-five verses written in Hausa and therefore targeted at the newly converted or immature student. It begins with repeated mantras, "Muhammada" or "Ahmada" (Muhammad's heavenly name):

Let us thank the Everlasting God
Praise be to the King who created Muhammad
Let us forever invoke blessings and peace
Upon the Prophet who excels all others, Ahmada
Accept the song of praise I shall sing
Accept, O people, let us praise Ahmada. (vv. 1–3)

The repetition of these terms provides a rhythmical accompaniment which can engage the attention of even a small child. Thus the needs of the beginner were met. However, despite the simplicity of the exercise, the constant repetition of these sacred words—Muhammada and Ahmada—is thought to bring the Prophet close to believers who recite them. The Prophet is with his community when they recite these words, which bring them closer to an experience of the Divine, through the utterance of words that evoke the sacred. Thus the recitation of a poem like *In Praise of Ahmada* can be called a "sacramental" experience.[7]

However, in this poem, Asma'u wove into her stanzas imagery that was directly borrowed from the great thirteenth-century poet al-Busiri. Translated from Arabic into Hausa and refashioned, they were recognizable touches of scholarship which indicated to other scholars Asma'u's own depth of scholarship. The recognition of other works within the context of her own poems enhanced the respectability of her works, casting them in the same league as the classics.

There are many examples of this technique in Asma'u's works. For example, al-Busiri's (d. 1296) *The Mantle*, a panegyric in praise of the Prophet, describes Muhammad's sacred, sweet olfactory aura: "No perfume can equal the dust on his bones" (v. 58). Similarly, in *In Praise of Ahmada* Asma'u writes, "Musk and myrrh do not equal / The perfume emitted by the body of Muhammad" (v. 13). In the *Mantle* al-Busiri writes of the portents that preceded the birth of Muhammad, which included the extinguishing of the sacred fire of the idolaters and the routing of scores of devils and evil spirits: "On that day the Persians perceived / Warnings of retribution and impending doom . . . / Sawa suffered when its lake ran dry (vv. 60, 64). Similarly, in *In Praise of Ahmada* Asma'u states: the "dying of the Persian fire is another example [foretelling his birth] / As is the river of Sawa which dried up because of Ahmada" (v. 21).

The Mantle appears in other of Asma'u's poems as well. The following example from *The Mantle* describes the fate of the enemies of the Prophet: "Vainly they hoped to flee, in envy almost of their slain / Whom eagles and vultures carried off in bits" (v. 120). This compares closely with Asma'u's description of the Gawakuke battlefield: "On that Tuesday paganism was overthrown / The corpses of their leaders were hacked to pieces / The vultures and hyenas said to each other, 'Who does this meat belong to?' / And they were told, 'It is yours. There is no need to squabble today'"

(*The Battle of Gawakuke*, vv. 54, 55). Such close re-creation of classic works is not only acceptable within the Arabic poetic mode, it is both a compliment to the original and an indication of the second author's mastery of the genre.[8]

Asma'u never patronized her students, but she provided in her works access to multiple layers of meaning at every level. Her works were replete with a wide variety of meanings hidden among features from the simplest to the most erudite, including clever vernacular wordplay, chapter and line citations from the Qur'an, and paraphrases from the classics. Through these techniques, Asma'u's students enjoyed a rich experience in reciting her poetry. For those unprepared for such techniques, her works provided the most basic of satisfactions by establishing for them mantras in the simple repetition of the rhymes. Asma'u recognized that in truly pious endeavors there is no room for intellectual elitism: she met each individual at his or her own level, in keeping with the Sufi tenets of humility and patient piety.

Doxologies

It is rare to find a work in the Arabic verse mode that lacks opening and closing doxologies to God. Just as Muslims begin any new endeavor by invoking God's name and aid, uttering, "*Bismillah Rahman, aRahim*" ("in the name of God, Most Gracious, Most Merciful"), poetic works are begun and ended in the same manner. The doxologies are the formulaic means of introducing and framing the work, as in this excerpt from Asma'u's *The Journey:*

> Let us thank God, the Almighty, for His generosity.
> It suffices us, brethren, let us praise Him.
> Let us invoke His blessing and God's peace upon our
>   Prophet,
> His family, Companions, and followers.
> Now I am going to explain the practice of the Shehu
> For you to hear what was done in his time. (vv. 1–3)

Asma'u's corpus of works indicates clearly her consummate skill in composition. She was too well educated and too talented to omit things by mistake. Where there are omissions, they must be considered intentional, aimed at creating a certain effect. Two of Asma'u's works are significant for their omission of opening doxologies, *Destroy Bawa* and *Ɗan Yalli*. In each case, the work is written in Fulfulde, so it is clearly intended for her kinsmen and not for the masses. Each is short, and written toward the end of her life (in 1861 and 1863, respectively), at a time when she must have been feeling frustrated with obstacles both without and within the Caliphate.

Destroy Bawa was composed in response to a raid by the enemy Bawa, a king of Gobir and descendant of the famous Bawa Jan Gwarzo, whom the Caliphate had been fighting for a decade. Asma'u was tired of his persistent threat; her irritation with him is evident in her emotional tone. The work is urgent, and the omission of doxology has a great deal to do with its efficacy as she gets right to the point:

> O God, destroy Bawa, son of our enemy, and humiliate
> Ɗan Balkore: O Lord let us hear news of their defeat.
> Cause their courage to fail and disperse them, confused
> and bewildered,
> For the sake of the Shehu our leader.[9] (vv. 1–2)

Similarly, in *Ɗan Yalli*, a work about a nearby leader and one of Asma'u's kinsmen, she does not hesitate to criticize without favoritism what she found to be corruption in her own family:

> Thanks be to God who empowered us to overthrow Ɗan
> Yalli
> Who has caused us so much trouble.
> He behaved unlawfully, he did wanton harm
> And caused hardship to Muslims. (vv. 1–2)

Given Asma'u's skill in composition, the omission of doxologies in these works gives insight into her personality, indicating not only her forthrightness and formidable nature, but the passion she felt on occasions that led her to express herself with urgency.

Manzuma

The versification of a pre-existing prose work is a technique called by the Arabic word *manzuma*. Asma'u was forty-three when her brother, Caliph Muhammad Bello, asked her to versify his work about Sufi women, *A Book of Good Advice* (*Kitab al-nasihah*). This volume is of considerable size (fifty folios), opening with a warning against acquisitiveness and a special caution about desire for gold and fine clothes. Bello wrote that the Prophet Muhammad told his wives that if they wanted lovely things, they should leave him and be divorced. Muhammad preached that women should be obedient to their husbands and give their clothes and finery as alms in order to escape the fires of Hell. Pure women, Muhammad said, were pious, upright, and frugal; he told his wife Aisha to love the very poor and care for them "because Allah will put you near them on the Day of the Resurrection of the Dead." Muhammad also said that a woman should only have the number of possessions that she could carry if she were making a journey on horseback. Bello's report on these observations occupy nine folios. Asma'u did not include them in her verse (*Sufi Women;* see appendix) on the same topic, but began her poem with a brief doxology of three verses followed by a statement of her aims:

> My aim in this poem is to tell you about Sufis
> To the great ones I bow in reverence
> I am mindful of them while I am still alive
> So that they will remember me on the Day of Resurrection
> The ascetic women are all sanctified
> For their piety they have been exalted
> They prayed ceaselessly to be delivered from the Fires of
>   Hell
> Take this to heart, my friends
> I have written this poem to assuage my heart:
> I remind you how they yearn for God. (vv. 4–8)

Asma'u's selective approach to the versification of Bello's work is a demonstration of her status and authority. In creating her own *Sufi Women* poem she did not merely translate her brother's work, but reshaped it to reflect a different emphasis on women's roles. Her poem incorporates the names of ascetic Sufi women, omits admonitions, and emphasizes the positive aspects of their practical, pious work in the world. Whereas Bello wrote seven folios about the Prophet's dutiful daughter Fadima, Asma'u said only, "And Fadima Zahra'u, or Batulu [her nickname] / Gracious lady, close follower of the Prophet. She was peerless, she who shunned the world / The

Prophet's daughter who was better than any other child" (vv. 16–17). Furthermore, Asma'u added to Bello's text by calling on women Sufi saints whom she recognized as extraordinary human beings:

> I pray, O God, for their blessings
> Give me the grace to repent my sins
> Out of respect for their greatness I dedicate myself
> Believing that I will receive what I request
> For their majesty will wipe away my sins
> And because of them I will escape the burden of my
>   wrongdoings
> In this world and the next where souls await judgment
> I will rely on them for my salvation. (vv. 57–60)

Moving beyond Bello's treatment of this topic, Asma'u transformed this into a poem not only about women, but also for the benefit of her women companions. She personalized the subject of Sufi women, whose "majesty will wipe away my sins . . . I will rely on them for my salvation" (vv. 59–60). These words do not appear in Bello's book, and the concept of invoking the help of women Sufi saints is unusual in the extreme. The fact that both editions of Asma'u's poem, in Hausa and Fulfulde, appeared during Bello's lifetime shows that he accepted and authorized her translations. Asma'u molded the material before her, demonstrating her mastery over the classic texts—including those by Bello—and the freedom to create a new work from them.

Asma'u's Sufism, piety, and good deeds made her an admirable person, but her literary skills and her ability to compose effectively in several languages spread her fame among the educated and illiterate alike. She was not only famous among the Muslim scholars in her community and beyond,[10] but she was also loved by ordinary unschooled villagers because she offered them, in languages they could understand, a place in Paradise with the Shehu through the works she composed. She also faced them with a horrific alternative to the rewards of piety: eternal hellfire, vividly described. In addition to religious instruction and enlightenment, Asma'u's poetic works offered views on recent history, with which they were familiar, and practical tools for their participation in a community newly unified under Islam.

She was renowned for her literary talent, but that was not an end in and of itself. Asma'u used her skills to promote the spread of Islam among everyone, regardless of ethnicity, language, literacy skills, gender, social status, or nationality. She was respected by scholars as far away as Mauritania and cherished within her own community. Her poetry demonstrates that she was a strong-willed woman, engaged in her cause, the unification of a Muslim state, in addition to being a poet sensitive to matters of grief and loss. She never wrote in isolation, but always was an activist, whose writings were merely instruments in bringing her fellow citizens to a higher good.

Sokoto as Medina: Imitating the Life of the Prophet and Re-enacting History

Five Nana Asma'u's works offer a rare firsthand historical account of the mission of the Sokoto jihad. The Shehu's campaign to revive Islam was viewed by political factions outside the Caliphate very differently from those in the community, but it had religious impetus rooted in, and it derived credibility from, the historical origins of Islam. The model for the Sokoto jihad was that of the Prophet Muhammad's own seventh-century campaign to promote Islam. That this was the Shehu's model is not surprising, since one of the guiding principles of Islam is following the *Sunna,* imitating the life of the Prophet.[1] Asma'u's works demonstrate that comparison of the Shehu with the Prophet was intentional; such comparison gave credibility to the jihad and the Shehu's actions in his campaign.

Of Asma'u's longest poems, one is an account of the life of the Prophet Muhammad and another is about the Shehu. Asma'u's intention in them is to connect the two historical figures for the purpose of imbuing the nineteenth-century jihad with the same positive spirit felt in the initial spread of Islam in the seventh century. Explicit in her views and firm in her mode of expression, Asma'u wrote confidently for the illumination and inspiration of the Muslim community, which included both devout, scholarly Muslims and new converts whose impressions were still malleable. Asma'u's parallels, linking the life and aims of the jihad leader Shehu Usman dan Fodiyo with those of the Prophet Muhammad, make a powerful vindication of the Shehu's credibility and authority in his nineteenth-century revivalist movement. Though the two men were separated by continents and centuries[2] the Shehu was, in his own lifetime, a towering figure because he reflected the Prophet's glory.

Yearning for the Prophet (see appendix) describes aspects of the Prophet Muhammad's life, while *The Journey* (see appendix) describes comparable aspects of the Shehu's life twelve centuries later. References to the similarities between the two men also are evident in other of Asma'u's works,[3] as well as in works by the Shehu himself and other illustrious figures of the day.[4] The scholarly community of the period would have been eminently aware of such parallels because they were steeped in the history of the Prophet and believed the evidence of their own eyes. But it was the scholar Asma'u who brought this knowledge to the level of ordinary people by writing it in Hausa, so that they could understand it when they heard it. To do this she employed a form known as *sira*, biography of the Prophet, a firmly established Arabic literary genre.[5] *Sira* works were created as a means of preserving historical knowledge, and they made up a significant part of the corpus of works that any Muslim scholar would likely have studied.

Al-Busiri's panegyric of the Prophet, *The Mantle*, was popular in the region. This work was appreciated in West Africa not only for its literary merits and for its devotional use, but also because it could serve as a sort of talisman.[6] *The Mantle* was widely distributed in the Muslim world, from Malaya to Mauretania, inspiring numerous poetic expansions (*takhmis*),[7] one of which was composed by Muhammad Bello in 1822, when Asma'u was twenty-nine years old. The Shehu himself wrote a panegyric on the Prophet, which his brother Abdullahi reworked as his own piece by adding lines as *takhmis*. When the Shehu translated this poem into Fulfulde with the title *Ma'ama'are* ("Yearning for the Prophet"), the work became famous. Its Hausa version, translated by Asma'u's brother Isa in 1864, became part of the repertoire of songs sung at mosques.[8] It is significant that the leaders of the community at Degel and later Sokoto wrote simultaneously in Arabic and the indigenous languages such as Hausa and Fulfulde. Asma'u would have studied these works as part of her cultural and literary education. Beginning with this classical *sira* form, Asma'u then added her own layer of historical significance concerning the Shehu and Bello. She saw nothing as coincidental, and strove to make others see the Shehu and Bello as the living saints she felt them to be. She gave credibility to their opposition to the enemy, both theological and military.

Another poet in Ɗegel who influenced Asma'u was one of the Shehu's own students, Muhammad Tukur.[9] His monumental 1789 work, *The Bringers of Good Tidings (Busuraa'u)*, is a praise poem for the Prophet Muhammad. It contains numerous references to the Prophet's life and his role in the Hereafter, and each of these verses ends with his name, Muhammad, or the alternative form Ahmed. It is twelve hundred verses long and takes six hours to be chanted. This work inspired another, shorter biographic poem by Tukur known as *Yearning for the Prophet (Begore)*, which tells also of the well-known happenings that occurred in Arabia at the time of the Prophet.[10] Details of the relationship between these two works by Tukur are not yet known, but it is *Yearning for the Prophet* which, as translated by Asma'u, has become more famous among Hausa-speaking women than any other of its genre, and which continues to have a public presence into the twenty-first century. Annually, at the time of the Prophet's birthday, crowds of women make a pilgrimage to Muhammad Tukur's tomb at Mutizgi, seventy miles south of Sokoto, an event which passes peacefully because it is well organized. Women have sung the song *Yearning for the Prophet* for more than 150 years, imparting the message to tens of thousands of people, and in the process wearing out their manuscript copies, which are handed down through the generations.

Asma'u's version of *Yearning for the Prophet* holds the same title and purpose as Tukur's: to preserve and recount Islamic history. Expanding this perspective is another work by Asma'u grounded in a caliphate context: *The Journey*. Asma'u's frequent allusions to the Qur'an and stories from the *hadith*s (stories about the Prophet's life) reinforce the more stunning parallels between the Shehu and the Prophet. *Yearning for the Prophet* functioned as a prism through which the Sokoto audience could view the life and work of the Shehu, set in comparison to the example of the Prophet. Following the *sira* style, *Yearning for the Prophet* focuses on battles and strategies in promoting Islam more than on the details of a life. Therefore this, like other such works, was conceived as a story of the life of the Prophet in relation to his missionary endeavors, rather than as the life of an individual. It was common in *sira* poetry to focus on military campaigns, yet these *sira* eventually became a means of expressing mystical philosophy as well. The parallels drawn between the Prophet's military strategies and those of the Shehu had the effect of bringing history to life for the Sokoto audience at the same time that they validated the contemporary efforts of the Shehu.

Yearning for the Prophet is accessible to both scholars and the uneducated, but at different levels. An understanding of the parallels between the two figures depends upon knowledge of both the life of the Prophet and the Shehu. A knowledgeable listener would need to have a grasp of the details of both men's lives. For the Sokoto populace this meant that teachers, specifically the *jajis*, carried the burden of undergoing training in the material, and then the responsibility of teaching it to an audience at the village level. Thus, history and religious knowledge were conveyed simultaneously with the politicization of the masses.

Yearning for the Prophet is a formidable work. Asma'u's version has 316 verses, takes about two hours to recite, and has its own talismatic properties. It has a rhyme which incorporates the names of the Prophet, Ahmada and Muhammada.[11] Even beginners could join in its recitation, and the constant repetition of the two names was a beneficial act of piety. Taken on its own, therefore, it is an important devotional work. For those who were still only elementary learners, the works themselves afford a talismanic atmosphere, allowing for the communal repetition of the name of the Prophet— "Muhammada," "Ahmada"—during the recitation of *Yearning for the Prophet*. Even if the listener missed the import of the overarching message, participation in the repetition of the end rhyme constituted a prayerful exercise, the performance of *dhikr*, Sufi prayer remembrance of God.

These two works by Asma'u—*Yearning for the Prophet* and *The Journey*—are powerful in the functions they fulfill on multiple levels. Historically, they authenticate an incipient theocracy, presenting the image of the Shehu as one who is doing the Prophet's work, following in his footsteps, enduring his difficulties, and expecting the same triumphant victory of Islam over its opponents. In the actual delivery, these works not only provide information, but function also as an opportunity for prayer. Surrounded by exemplary works, and because their author was committed to making her compositions relevant to her time, Asma'u's historical works taken together create for members of the community—both devout Muslims and new converts alike—a three-dimensional image of Islam as the prime determinant factor in their lives, and faith in the jihad as an unquestionable premise.

Asma'u believed the Shehu's life reflected the Prophet's intentionally, and she fashioned the poem about her father to bring out the likenesses. She did not manipulate the facts, but placed emphasis on points of convergence, underlining actions of her father Shehu that mirrored those of the Prophet. Asma'u's *The Journey* was meant to be used alongside *Yearning for the Prophet* to drive home to her audiences the impression of the jihad's divine inspiration.

She accomplished this by describing specific points of comparison between the two men and their campaigns: initial periods of proselytizing, a *hijra* and a battle against all odds, itinerancy, attack and desertion of troops, peace overtures, and unification signaling the successful end to the campaign.

A Comparative View of *Yearning for the Prophet* and *The Journey*

To begin with, the Shehu proselytized, like the Prophet, calling people to religion. The Prophet and the Shehu began their campaigns at about the same age. *Yearning for the Prophet* confirms that the Prophet Muhammad was thirty-five years old "when the Holy Spirits were made known to [him]" (v. 82). Sokoto audiences would have heard the Shehu say he was thirty-six years old when "God removed the veil from my eyes" (Hiskett 1973: 64–65). The Shehu's preaching took him from town to town, as Asma'u reports in *The Journey:*

> You should know that he called people to Islam in Ɗegel,
> And also at Dauran, and there at Faru, through his zeal.
> He turned northward, proselytizing
> Until all the people answered his call.
> He returned home to Ɗegel and then went
> On to the Niger, always giving his sermons.
> The Muslim community accepted his call everywhere,

Those of the east and west, because of his high standing.
He overthrew non-Islamic customs and
Established Muslim law. Let us follow his path. (vv. 6–10)

The specifics of the Prophet's preaching are more abbreviated, moving immediately to the opposition he faced.

When he was forty
Plus a day, God sent to Ahmada
The Archangel Gabriel,
God sent the Qur'an to Ahmada.
Evil was overturned: those who practice it
Will never know even a tenth of the mysteries of Ahmada.
The way of saying prayers and ablution was sanctified:
People began to repeat them and follow Muhammada.
In the fourth year he began proselytizing.
The eyes of unbelievers were closed because they refused
   to respond to Muhammada.
In the fifth year they [his followers] went to Abyssinia.
The Negus [Abyssinian ruler] treated them with consider-
   ation, because of Muhammada.
The unbelievers rose against Muhammada . . .
As Islam gained strength, the unbelievers came
With their complaints to the family of Muhammada.
(*Yearning for the Prophet*, vv. 85–91, 98)

Just as the Ethiopians embraced Islam introduced by the Prophet, so too the people on the Niger were converted by the Shehu.

Similarly, they both faced formidable opposition, which for each led to a *hijra*, or strategic retreat, to prepare for battle. The Shehu and his followers moved their encampment for safety:

Aliyu Jeɗo went there to Gudu with
Mahmud Gurdam where they prepared a camp for the
   Shehu.
Then Agali came,
He carried the Shehu's things, and his books.
On the twelfth day of the month of Zulkida
Our Shehu made his *hijra*. (*The Journey*, vv. 15–17)

Asma'u recited the names of the places at which they halted, each one imprinted on her memory.

On Thursday he took the road to Kwaren Geza,
To Demba, and Kalmalo; one after the other.
At Farkaji he slept, and at Ruwawuri,
At Gudu God gave him lodging, him and his people.
(*The Journey*, vv. 18–19)

Asma'u's account of the retreat is precise, reminding the listener of unforgettable dangers. Her description of the Prophet's retreat follows the well-known accounts of the Prophet's life, which was also fraught with difficulties:

In the twelfth year he journeyed to Heaven
And five prayers a day were instituted by Muhammada. . . .
In one year when fealty was given at Akaba
Twelve men went to Ahmada. . . .
In the fourteenth year he made his *Hijra* to Medina
And his enemies came to destroy Muhammada.
He entered a cave with [Abubakar]
No one discovered the hiding place of Ahmada. . . .
In that place it was as dry as dust
And no help except God's—who loved Muhammada.
(*Yearning for the Prophet*, vv. 105, 107, 112–113, 115)

Asma'u makes clear that both the Prophet and the Shehu initially had to retreat from the opposition, and that God was the one who best helped them, guaranteeing their safety. The Prophet was transported to Heaven in the twelfth year of his campaign to confer with God; on the twelfth day of the month, the Shehu made his *hijra*.[12] These comparable references would have been significant to Asma'u's audience.

Like the Prophet, the Shehu engaged in battles following the organization of his followers in exile. The Battle of Badr was the Prophet's first battle (A.D. 624); it was so significant in the Prophet's campaign to establish Islam that the names of the warriors who died in it are used as reverently as those of other prophets mentioned in the Qur'an, the Prophet Muhammad's Companions, and Muhammad himself (Schimmel 1994: 121). The first great battle of the Sokoto jihad, at Tabkin Kwatto, was captained by Abdullahi, the Shehu's brother, who linked the victory at Kwatto to the events which happened at Badr when he said, "I saw their waterless cloud had cleared away from the sun of Islam which was shining, by the help of Him who helped the Prophet against the foe at Badr."[13] That single word, "Badr," evokes in the listener a plethora of related terms, endowing the subject with reverence and veneration. The uninitiated, of course, would have to be taught the significance of the key words and phrases, but once the connections were made, the implication that these battles were comparable would be clear. At both Badr and Kwatto it was God, not superior forces, that guaranteed the victories of the Muslims:

> There were nine hundred
> And fifty of the enemy at Badr when they met Ahmada.
> The Muslims were three hundred and ten
> And three, only they were with Ahmada. . . .
> The Angels of Gabriel were the warriors of Muhammada.
> (*Yearning for the Prophet*, vv. 123–124, 127)

> At the battle of Kwatto, the Haɓe [enemy] were in disarray
> They never returned again to attack him at his open
>   encampment. (*The Journey*, v. 31)

In each case, it is being on the side of right that leads to victory in battle.[14]

Desertion was a problem in both the Prophet's Battle of Uhud and the Shehu's battle against the Gobir-Tuareg alliance of 1805. In each case, the Muslim forces were vastly outnumbered. At Uhud the Meccan enemy had mobilized a force of three thousand, while the Prophet had only seven hundred men. At Gwandu the jihad forces faced a large camel-mounted army of Tuaregs that had joined with the army of powerful Gobir. A Qur'anic verse tells the story of what happened at the Prophet's Battle of Uhud in the third year of the *Hijra*, A.D. 625. It describes the disobedience of the Prophet's men, who defied orders and left their posts to join the pursuit of the enemy in order to gain booty:

> God did indeed fulfill
> His promise to you
> When ye with His permission
> Were about to annihilate
> Your enemy—until ye flinched
> And fell to disputing
> About the order

And disobeyed it
After He brought you in sight
[Of the booty] which ye covet.
Among you are some
That hanker after this world
And some that desire
The Hereafter. Then did He
Divert you from your foes
In order to test you.
But He forgave you:
For God is full of grace
To those who believe. (3: 152)

Asma'u describes desertion at the Battle of Uhud almost in code. Those familiar with the Qur'an and the story of the Prophet would have had no difficulty making the link with what happened at Gwandu.

When dawn broke they were at Uhud
Where the unbelievers met with Muhammada.
The Muslims made their headquarters at I'nina
To kill the unbelievers who had shunned Ahmada.
Look at the ranks of young men
Who, like Hamza, were killed in front of Ahmada.
(*Yearning for the Prophet,* vv. 142–144)

The deserters were the "unbelievers who had shunned Ahmada," but the day was saved by the heroism of a few, most of whom, like the valorous Hamza, met their deaths. The graves may still be seen at the site of Uhud, three miles north of Medina.

In 1805 near Gwandu the huge enemy force marched toward the Shehu's camp, whereupon his forces took up defensive positions to the northeast. But before the enemy arrived, a group of his men attacked a friendly village for booty. Their action weakened the defense, and for five days the Shehu's army was forced to retreat:

The community gave battle and Hammadi
Obtained martyrdom shortly after his arrival there.
So the men fled,
He alone remained, and everybody knows of his valor.
(*The Journey,* vv. 78–79)

The Shehu's brother, Abdullahi, called the booty seekers and deserters a "rabble of young hooligans," but all were consoled by the fact that centuries earlier in Arabia it had happened before.[15]

In instructing her *jajis* Asma'u filled in the details and answered their questions concerning the battle. She also took the opportunity to bring home to her students the lessons to be learned from the disobedience of the deserters. The Qur'an is unequivocal on this issue:

> It was Satan
> Who caused them to fail
> Because of some [evil]
> They had done. (3: 155)

Asma'u made it clear that loyalty to the cause was the only option worthy of respect.[16] She also made explicit the fate of the enemies of truth. The Tuareg leader was "filled with fear and terror—God, the Almighty King, overthrew him" (*The Journey*, vv. 81, 83).

Asma'u drew more parallels, even to the point of citing the same place names for certain battles. Such coincidence had to carry a great deal of significance:

> As Muhammad stepped forth he had no more than three
>   thousand men.
> At Salah was the war camp of Muhammada.
> They stayed there twenty-four days waiting for the battle
>   to commence. (*Yearning for the Prophet*, vv. 169–170)

Mount Salah is an outcropping of rock to the northwest of Medina. But that was not the point. What Asma'u was doing was reminding people that her brother, Muhammad Bello, had made his war camp at a place they called Salah, near Gwandu. Asma'u herself was at Salah with her husband, waiting until all Bello's allies had arrived. He then set out to conquer the enemy capital, Alkalawa. The battle is described in *The Journey:*

> The army he [the Shehu] sent to Gobir
> Was joined by every man of note.
> After he had completed the preparations
> He captured Alkalawa. (*The Journey*, vv. 88, 89)

Asma'u's audience at the time would have known that the Alkalawa battle involved Bello's encampment at Salah, and would have drawn a connection between it and the Prophet's encampment of the same name.

The end results of the Prophet's and the Shehu's campaigns are clearly comparable. With victory came capitulation to the social order inherent in Islam. The success of the Prophet's battle victories and campaign resulted in a groundswell of support for Islam as a religion, a social order, and a political framework: "The whole population began to come / Town by town they entered the religion of Ahmada" (*Yearning for the Prophet*, v. 251). There follows a long list of the tribes that joined the Prophet's side, and constituted the first unification of Muslim peoples. The Shehu enjoyed a similar victory and a comparable unification of peoples in a vast region:

> Victory was obtained in every quarter, . . .
> When people heard the Shehu's call to religion they all
> came
> From north, west, east and south, for his sake.
> (*The Journey*, vv. 101–102)

The territorial areas listed included a vast region of present-day Nigeria, including Nupe, Western Bornu, Yorubaland, Bauci, and Kano. The victory was significant in establishing reformed Islam as a guiding sociopolitical force in the region.

During the stability that followed warfare the Prophet established an Islamic state. He appointed law keepers and ambassadors, accepted the repentance of enemies, and guided the progress of those serving the needs of the state:

> He sent emissaries to Yemen and Azerbaijan
> And appointed judges, Muhammada.
> He sent messages to Jariru at Zulkira
> Demanding he repent and end disputing with Ahmada. . . .
> He planned and sent an expedition to Amyaku
> To revenge the defeat of Zaidu who loved Muhammada.
> (*Yearning for the Prophet*, vv. 286–287, 292)

Similarly, the Shehu moved actively from warfare to community; he appointed caretakers and officials to ensure the stability of the state:

> Borno was defeated and given to Zaki, and Maude to Dan
>   Goni Mukhtari,
> The Shehu gave them both office because of the help they
>   had given him.
> Sulaiman was given the emirship of Kano,
> Ishaq was given Daura.
> And Sambo, son of Ashafa who helped him,
> He was given 'Yandoto in Zamfara as his portion. . . .
> The Shehu divided responsibility [for the territories]: the
>   west to his brother;
> The eastern part to Bello his son.
> (*The Journey*, vv. 91–93, 97)

Having built their nations, both men died; Asma'u, following convention, speaks but briefly about their deaths. Of the Prophet she said, "Well you know that for twelve days / He was sick, then he passed away, Ahmada" (v. 298), and of the Shehu she said:

> The Shehu left there [Gwandu] and settled at Sifawa.
> Opportunity and prosperity increased. . . .
> One Monday [in 1815] he came to Sokoto
> And he spent two years there.
> Then he passed on to the next world, In the month of
>   Jimada
> It was on the third of the month.
> (*The Journey*, vv. 99, 105–106)

Thus the stories of the Prophet's and the Shehu's campaigns to promote Islam and reform those around them were merged. Asma'u intentionally selected comparable events in her accounts, making quite clear the parallels between the two important figures.

Many poets before this had been commissioned by princes to write verse, or summoned before fashionable gatherings to read their compositions. In Asma'u's case neither applied. It is suggested here that she had three motives: she wrote to educate the masses, to explain and defend the jihad, and to further illuminate the illustrious character of the Shehu. She was, of course, aware of the political importance of her actions: anyone who accepted the facts as she presented them could only conclude that God was on the side of the Shehu. Therefore to oppose him was to oppose God and the Prophet, a position beyond any hope of redemption. This was a high-stakes endeavor. Hints of the strain that Asma'u was under as she strove to write interlinking poetry on such momentous and politically sensitive issues, and on such a grand scale, are found in *Yearning for the Prophet:*

> Do not leave me by myself . . .
> Please go on helping me . . .
> . . . oh! listen to what I have to tell you about Ahmada. . . .
> Bring water to refresh me as I faint.
> Today I weary, longing so much for Muhammada.
> (*Yearning for the Prophet,* vv. 240, 258, 260)

The message was aimed at every level of society, every ethnic group, an intention evidenced by the fact that these poems were written in languages ordinary people could understand, Fulfulde and Hausa, the tongues spoken in the marketplace and at the family hearth. In these works Asma'u reached out to the populace, not only to the intelligentsia.

The Sokoto jihad was founded on the belief that society should be shaped in imitation of the earliest Muslim community. While those outside the Caliphate perceived the campaign through a political lens, the views of the Caliphate community members were focused on Islam. Politics and religion had to be inextricably intertwined as the driving force of the jihad, and the creation of a caliphal theocracy, but the insider's view of the jihad was that it was divinely motivated and those who were instrumental in its promotion sought to draw the vanquished into its ranks. Asma'u's works attest to the integrity of the impetus for the Sokoto jihad, a watershed movement that changed forever the sociopolitical nature of the region.

Caliphate Women's Participation
in the Community

Six A certain number of women in the Caliphate community, like their descendants in contemporary Sokoto and nearby towns,[1] were teachers and writers. In the predominantly oral culture of the Caliphate, teachers were effective in transmitting works through the spoken, chanted word. Repetition and memorization of these popular poems resulted in their reaching a far wider audience than originally intended, as voices echoed beyond the open-air class area and recitations passed well beyond the first learners to the extended family and neighbors alike. Asma'u established a cadre of literate, itinerant women teachers (*jaji*s) who disseminated her instructive poetic works among the masses. Trained by Asma'u, these women were extension teachers, using Asma'u's works as lesson plans and mnemonic devices through which they instructed secluded women in the privacy of their homes.[2] The tradition of educating women, and of women themselves writing tracts as practical guides to both rudimentary life skills and pious behavior, was an integral part of the Sokoto Caliphate community. The practice continues into the twenty-first century.[3] In nearly every case, contemporary women cite Nana Asma'u as their exemplar in seeking knowledge as a necessary pursuit in their lives.[4] This was a matter which she said could be undertaken only if they behaved like respectable married women.

Nana Asma'u's training of *jaji*s and the *'yan-taru* was community work whose primary tool was the spoken word. In keeping with the attitude of reverence for the word that lies at the heart of Islam, her scholarship and dissemination of it were expressive of

Figure 6.1. Girl reading from an allo

the spirit of Islam in both content and form. Not all her poetic verse was theological tract, but all of it was relevant to some layer of the community, whether scholarly or unschooled. Captured Hausa men and women were new in the Caliphate, and needed to know practical things: how to dress, how to pray, how to reshape the common details of their lives into Islamic form. Asma'u's works not only informed women on these matters, but also reinforced Sufi characteristics and the principles of the *Sunna* by outlining in praise poems the spirituality and moral characteristics that made a person noteworthy. It was not a person's wealth or political achievements that were significant, but faith and right living. Asma'u cites the asceticism and teaching skills of long-dead Sufi women, and the benevolent characteristics of her brother Bello, the caliph, as examples to be followed. The message she conveys in these works is that worldly greatness is not a worthy aim, but personal goodness—patience and generosity—is what makes a person pious.

Al-Ghazali's (A.D. 1058–1111)[5] treatise *On the Duties of Brotherhood,* a classic work with which Asma'u was familiar,[6] advises the devout Muslim on eight specific obligations toward his or her community members: material assistance, personal aid, holding one's tongue, speaking out, forgiveness, prayer, loyalty and sincerity, and affording relief from discomfort and inconvenience. Concern for the material, psychological, and spiritual welfare of the community was incumbent upon every individual, and was the guiding principle of society. Attention to these issues was integrated with the advocation of the *Sunna,* the right mode of behavior, as the focus of the community. In short, there was much that a woman not only *could* do, but was *obligated* to do in the promotion of the good of the community, and for the good of her own soul. These are the principles that Asma'u and her students promoted in the community, and women's roles were central to their promotion. By teaching women, Asma'u was by extension training whole families in orthodox Sufi practices that focused on following the *Sunna* and the Qur'an, the two guiding lights of the Caliphate.

Growing up as she did during the jihad instilled in Asma'u an activist spirit that gave no quarter to elitist approaches to literary works. Each of her long poems is functional well beyond the promotion of the aesthetic. The works discussed here demonstrate the kinds of "lesson plans" she created for *'yan-taru.* As mnemonic devices, these works could be memorized by teachers and students and then explained in fuller detail during instruction. *The Path of Truth, A Warning, II* (see appendix), and *Sufi Women* (see appendix) are some of the best examples of the ways in which Asma'u used her scholarship to spread knowledge and provide benefit to the entire community. *Lamentations for Aisha, I & II* (see appendix) and elegies for Zaharatu, Hawa'u, and Fadima describe exemplary lives of women.

These works function in different yet complementary ways. They share attention to the community of women, whether Fulani or Hausa, whether seasoned scholars or novices. *The Path of Truth* provides both basic and theologically sophisticated instruction in Islam that is useful to either women or men. *A Warning, II* couches instruction in terms of advocating proper behavior, in both practical action (the pillars of Islam) and attention to the spirit behind activity, such as attending classes outside the home. *Sufi Women* connects the community of caliphate women to Muslim women scholars and Sufis throughout history, confirming a tradition of women as active members of the devout Muslim community over twelve centuries, while *Lamentations for Aisha, I & II* and elegies for various women present examples of women whose characters bear imitation.

The Path of Truth

When a *jaji* left Asma'u to return to her home village, she walked in the midst of her group of women students, her distinguishing headgear lending utmost respectability to the group. She probably carried a copy of Asma'u's latest work, which may well have been at one time *The Path of Truth*. Written in Hausa in 1842, it has one hundred thirty-two verses, divided into sections treating obligatory religious duties, resurrection, sinners, salvation, and Paradise, which merits three consecutive sections at the end. All this is framed by opening and closing prayer doxologies. Each couplet's end rhyme provides a mantra: the repetition of "Ahmada" or "Muhammada" every two lines keeps the work focused on the need to follow the *Sunna,* the example of the Prophet Muhammad.

Following the opening doxology (nine verses), the next section describes in detail the obligations of the pillars of Islam, as well as outlining the obligations and attitudes of Sufi living. Throughout these twenty verses neither male nor female is mentioned. Rather it is emphasized repeatedly that these obligations are incumbent upon every Muslim:

> You should always be clean and wear clean clothes.
> Look well to the details of your religion so that we may all
>   be united with Ahmada.
> You should seek religious knowledge and stop straying from
> The Path. Do not be one of the lost in the next world.
>   Ahmada.
> Such knowledge enables you to follow God and the
>   Prophet.
> Insight into the *Sunna* will carry us to Ahmada.
> Wishing for a Muslim everything that you
> Wish for yourself is [in keeping with] the character of
>   Muhammada. (vv. 19–21, 28)

One can well imagine this section being used to instruct those new to the orthodox practice of Islam, informing them of the practical details of daily Muslim behavior.

In the next section, eleven couplets describe examples of inappropriate behavior. Like every culture, this one had to deal with usurers, adulterers, slanderers, hypocrites, liars, show-offs, frauds, and intriguers. These sinners are described like figures in a Hieronymus Bosch painting, suffering the fates they have earned:

> The usurers will see their bellies swell bigger than gourds
> In size and exposed to Ahmada.
> They will rise on the Last Day as if possessed of the Devil
> The Qur'an told their fate, Ahmada.
> The stink of the adulterer is worse than the stench of
>   carrion:
> He will be driven away, so that he is far from Ahmada.
> The slanderer, the hypocrite
> And he who gives false witness will not see Ahmada.
> With their tongues hanging down to their chests, they will
>   be exposed
> For they will not get salvation from Ahmada. (vv. 40–44)

Likewise the arrogant, the tyrannous, the intriguer, the fraud, the embezzler and briber, the ungrateful child, the backbiter, the envious, thieves, and infidels will receive punishments appropriate to their sins. Asma'u makes clear that this plan, guaranteeing that "what goes around comes around," is not hers, but derives from the word of God, for the Qur'an told their fate (v. 41). This section aims to scare students into right behavior, reinforcing the instruction that precedes it with the sure result of failing to follow Muslim obligations.

The next thirteen verses are an instruction manual for the Day of Salvation. A series of events will signal the end of the world, beginning with Muhammad's return to earth:

> Muhammad will return and our deeds will be weighed
>   while we stand
> Some will be saved only through the salvation of Ahmada.
> Those whose [good] deeds exceed
> The bad ones will be saved only through the salvation of
>   Ahmada.

Those whose bad deeds exceed
On that day will perish, unless they are saved by Ahmada.
Papers will be given to some in the right hand, to others
In the left hand: the latter will be far away from Ahmada.
The meritorious will be saved because they followed
The way of the *Sunna* and helped Muhammada.
(vv. 60–64)

The plan is clear: it remains only for the student, the aspiring good Muslim, to follow the right path.

The second half of this work describes Paradise, its approach bridge, its pools, and those who will be lucky enough to populate it. To individuals in the Sokoto Caliphate, immersed in dusty, hot, difficult days, such a work had to be a welcome reprieve from the toils of the day, offering hope in the distant future, and the assurance that certain behavior in the present guaranteed the contentment Paradise had to offer:

Let us dwell there and drink milk and honey
And enjoy bliss together with Ahmada.
For there is no illness, no aging, no poverty
No death: we remain forever
Forever in enjoyment, relaxation and pleasant talk
We walk in Paradise, we have seen Muhammada.
(vv. 94–96)

Throughout each section of this long poem, there is a noticeable absence of gender bias. This perspective is in keeping with the belief in Sufism of the equitable position of men and women; the "soul has no gender." It is clear from other works by Asma'u that she is well aware of the importance of describing women's roles when appropriate, as will be discussed below. But this work is a carefully balanced account aimed at the good Muslim, and it is significant that she eschews the opportunity to use gender-specific pronouns. Indeed, the only ones used are in relation to the Prophet Muhammad; otherwise she speaks directly to *you*, i.e., her Muslim audience, without gender. Yet this work is not devoid of personal touches. At the end of the work, Asma'u wove into the verses the seal of her authority, speaking directly to her audience again as "friends":

If anyone asks who composed this song, say
That it is Nana, daughter of the Shehu, who loves
    Muhammada.
You should firmly resolve, friends, to follow her
And thus you will follow exactly the *Sunna* of
    Muhammada. (vv. 125–126)

Generations of women learned this poem by heart, and in doing so they internalized the message that right living is the aim of every Muslim; the *Sunna* is the Way, the Path of Truth.

A Warning, II

Other times created other needs. *A Warning, II* was written in 1856, in Hausa, for the benefit of the sections of the population needing resocialization and instruction in the guiding principles of the Caliphate. The Prophet instructed teachers to "speak to the people according to their understanding"; Asma'u would have been familiar with this advice. This work is appropriate to the time in terms of its message, its form, and its mode of delivery. The message is a simple, direct outline of the tenets to be followed by orthodox Muslims; the form is the couplet, and the language is that of the masses, Hausa. As in the longer work *The Path of Truth,* Asma'u explains here—in only twenty-seven couplets—the basic principles of Islam for anyone whose level of devotion was questionable: follow the pillars of Islam and the *Sunna*. The first nineteen couplets are a distillation of the longer work in setting forth the obligations of devout Muslims.

It is significant that Asma'u focuses on women in the next five verses, spending nearly a fifth of the entire work directly addressing women who are new to the Muslim caliphate community. These "women's verses" are liberating. This may surprise feminists who are "apt to be suspicious towards Islam which they consider a sexist tool of oppression" (Coulon 1988: 114) and those historians who believe the Shehu "insisted on secluding Muslim women."[7] We know from the Shehu's own writings on the subject that many of the educated elite wanted their wives to stay at home but failed to teach them anything, treating them "like household implements which became broken after long use and which are then thrown out on the dung heap."[8] In this context, therefore, Asma'u's words are very significant for she says that women have a duty to seek knowledge, which by implication means taking the initiative and acting according to their consciences. She said, "Seek," not "Wait until someone does something for you," and, yes, she said women must obey their husbands, but only their lawful demands.

> Women, a warning. Leave not your homes without good
>   reason
> You may go out to get food or to seek education.
> In Islam, it is a religious duty to seek knowledge
> Women may leave their homes freely for this.
> Repent and behave like respectable married women
> You must obey your husbands' lawful demands.
> You must dress modestly and be God-fearing.
> Do not imperil yourselves and risk hell-fire.
> Any woman who refuses, receives no benefit,
> The merciful Lord will give her the reward of the damned.
> (vv. 20–24)

But wherever there are obligations there are also rights. This work states clearly that if a woman wants freedom it has got to be in the context of behaving as an exemplary Muslim. Discreetly dressed women may "leave their homes freely" for education; in fact, they "must" go out to seek education—it is their religious obligation to do so. The work's emphasis on seeking religious knowledge is significant in promoting *among women* the ethos of spirituality based on intellectual pursuit of an understanding of God, and the intention is that such spiritual knowledge will benefit the entire community. Indeed, the last verse before the closing doxology confirms that this is Asma'u's intention in this poem:

> I have written this poem of admonition
> For you to put to good use in the Community. (v. 25)

Women were required to contribute to the promotion of the socio-spiritual needs of the Sokoto Caliphate.

Sufi Women

That women have had such an active role to play in the Muslim community was not a new idea to Asma'u. Educated in a classic

Islamic mode, she was familiar with works such as thirteenth-century Ibn al-Jawzi's *Sifat al-safwa,* which lists Sufi women saints of exemplary character. Asma'u's brother Bello wrote on the topic in an effort to remind people of the Sufi foundation of the Qadiriyya community,[9] warning women to harken back to the Sufi principles and urging them to eschew their acquisitiveness. His work is founded on older works, such as that of al-Jawzi, which described Sufi women saints as "blessed anonymous women who gave themselves over to perpetual worship" (Chodiewicz 1994: 18).[10]

With evident enthusiasm, Asma'u seized Bello's composition, translating it into both Hausa and Fulfulde verse within a few months, thus making it available to as wide an audience as possible, but Asma'u's poem is not simply a reworking of earlier sources, for she makes it relevant to her community in several ways. It includes transmogrified versions of the Arabic names of women, making them more accessible to her own community. For instance the historical Habiba 'Adawiyah becomes Habibatu Adawiyyatu in Asma'u's version, and the famous eighth-century Sufi woman saint Rabi'a of Basra appears as Rabia'tul in the Hausa-Fulani version of her name. It is certain that Asma'u was aware of the original Arabic names—so well known was al-Jawzi's work, and so classic was Asma'u's education. Therefore, Asma'u's decision to localize them indicates her intention of making this work relevant to her own audience. Asma'u describes the wives of the Prophet (vv. 11–15, 21), his mother and daughters, and also the women of the community of her father, the Shehu. Two of his wives were still alive at the time of the composition of the poems; she described them as exceedingly pious, unworldly, good-natured, and generous.[11] Other Caliphate women were renowned scholars:

> The teacher of women, Habiba
> She was most revered and had great presence.
> I speak of Aisha, a saint
> On account of her asceticism and determination.
> And Joda Kowuuri, a Qur'anic scholar
> Who used her scholarship everywhere. . . .
> There were others who were upright
> In the community of the Shehu; I have not listed them.
> Very many of them had learned the Qur'an by heart

And were exceedingly pious and zealous.
(*Sufi Women*, vv. 68–70, 73–74)

These images indicate a continued, accepted presence of women teachers in the Caliphate community. More importantly, such a presence is modeled on women's roles that extend back to the period of the establishment of Islam, and Asma'u weaves into her work evidence of the historical precedent for such roles.

The poem *Sufi Women* emphasizes that pious women are to be seen in the mainstream of Islam, and to warn against excessive attachment to worldly gain. It could be memorized by teachers for instructional purposes. Its intended effect was to mobilize women in promoting the Muslim ethos over all other authorities. Thus, in response to the application of political or patriarchal pressure, women could cite this poem as support for their insistence on spiritual over human laws.

Asma'u's versions of *Sufi Women* are, in the Islamic world, rare examples of "popular" women's history. Written for ordinary house-wives, the poems had the potential to transform their lives by giving them a sense of identity and ridding them of the despair which rootlessness brings. Importantly, Asma'u affirmed her personal belief in the power of the great saints of womankind. In a remarkable and possibly unique way she said she looked to them, personally, for help.

> For their majesty will wipe away my sins
> And because of them I will escape the burden of my
> wrongdoings.
> In this world and the next, where souls await judgment
> I will rely on them for my salvation. (vv. 59–60)

In this she speaks for all women who might have heard this work, placing herself among the ranks of ordinary women of the caliphate, subject to the same doubts, worries, and burdens.

Lamentations for Aisha, I & II

The elegy was a standard genre of poetic expression, in which Asma'u excelled, proving to be one of the most prolific lament writers of her time. She wrote between sixteen and twenty elegies.[12] Some are in praise of revered figures like Bello, her uncle Abdullahi, or the famed scholar Mustapha, but six focus on the lives of women who might otherwise have remained unknown to history. She held deep respect for everyone who lived a useful life in the context of Islam and expressed her appreciation of their efforts in what she wrote. To her, Halima, "a kind neighbor," and Zaharatu, who with willingness "attended women in childbirth," made contributions which were necessary and highly valued.

The two works that she wrote for Aisha, her lifelong friend and eventual sister-in-law, should be read as a pair because they express complementary perspectives on mourning. The first describes Aisha's accomplishments as a devout Muslim who cared for orphans and widows, promoted community harmony, and possessed the piety of one who has memorized the Qur'an. In this work Asma'u appeals to God to preserve Aisha's soul and welcome her into His eternal light. The second work is more heartfelt. In it Asma'u offers insight into the ways in which these women related to one another, neither isolated nor under the domination of men. The depth of Asma'u's grief is evident in this work:

> This poem was written because there is no one else like her
>   from among the Brethren. How long my nights dwell
>   on her.
> How often she helped me to forget my own grief
>   and how often she helped me most kindly.
> The depth of my sadness and loneliness after her death has
>   grown
> O the multitude of my sorrows, the deepening of my
>   gloom! (*Lamentation for Aisha, II*, vv. 5–7)

Asma'u notes that although wild expressions of grief are eschewed, crying and like mourning is not forbidden in Islam: "I cry for her with tears of compassion / and of longing and sympathy for her, and loving friendship" (*Lamentation for Aisha, II*, v. 14).

Asma'u's loss is also a loss for the community, because Aisha was so active and contributed so much to it: "She was a guardian of orphans and widows / a pillar of the community, ensuring harmony" (*Lamentation for Aisha, I*, v. 8). Having memorized the Qur'an and by implication being as learned as many a judge, Aisha was as able to clarify the inheritance rights of widows and orphans as to find them shelter, food, and clothing. As wife of the Caliph she was able to champion any cause from a position of strength. She was accessible to women in need, and listened to what they had to say.

In the second work lamenting Aisha's death, Asma'u is colloquial and heartfelt:

> Oh my eyes weep liberally for my loved one
> as a consolation for my grief and a companion for my
> gloom.
> Shed copious tears for the loss of Aisha
> the noblest of my dear ones of my age group, my
> friend. . . .
> The depth of my sadness and loneliness after her death has
> grown
> O the multitude of sorrows, the deepening of my gloom!
> Know you not that love, when firmly established, is
> priceless?
> There is no child who could make me forget that love
> and no brother, nothing which could soothe me, not even
> all sorts of riches.
> Therefore my heart withers from worrying:
> sigh after sigh rises up from my grief;
> Tears have continued to flow constantly
> as if they would never dwindle or cease. . . .
> I cry for her with tears of compassion
> and of longing and sympathy for her, and loving friend-
> ship. (vv. 1–2, 7–11, 14)

Not only does Asma'u reveal her own humanity in mourning so deeply, but she also accepts Aisha's frailties: "[May God] forgive her lapses and reward her / for the good things she did for me gladly and graciously" (v. 17). Taken together, these two works on Aisha describe her many aspects, from formal to casual, and draw her fully as a three-dimensional woman whose presence is a loss to the community as well as to the individuals who knew and loved her.

Elegies for Fadima, Zaharatu, and Hawa'u

These are short works (23, 28, and 21 verses, respectively) in which the best-known traits of each woman are lauded. Each is praised in remembrance of the positive contributions she made to the community. The emphasis is not on who she was, but on how her actions defined the depth of her character. In each case, her actions are in accord with the spirit of the *Sunna* and the aims of the Muslim Sokoto community.

Fadima was Muhammad Bello's full- and Asma'u's half-sister and seems to have inherited the same kind of energy that he had:

> She succored the Community with her many acts of
> charity, feeding people.
> Relatives and strangers alike: she showed no discrimina-
> tion. She gave generously; she urged people to study.
> She produced provisions when an expedition was
> mounted. She had many responsibilities.
> She sorted problems and urged people to live peacefully,
> and forbade squabbling. (vv. 7–10)

Fadima married the army Commander in Chief, (the *amir al-jaish*), Aliyu Jedo; hence, her involvement with organizing the production of "hardtack" food for the army. Two principal items were *murje* and *kilishi*, the former a kind of muesli, the latter dried meat. Both were high-protein foods, light in weight and long-lasting. *Murje* was produced by first threshing and milling millet seeds, then cooking the millet flour, drying it, soaking it in butter and honey, drying it again, and finally rubbing it into granules which could be stored by a horseman in his saddlebags and either eaten as it came or reconstituted into porridge by the addition of milk. To prepare food like this would entail negotiations with all manner of suppliers, as well as the workforce. Fadima linked these activities with her famed hospitality, which had nothing to do with entertainment and everything to do with providing food on a daily basis for anyone who, at nightfall, was at the gates of the house and was hungry.[13]

Asma'u did not just confine her praise to women such as Fadima who performed prodigious tasks, but, as we have already stated, she also encouraged women by praising those who did quite mundane jobs. Zaharatu was such a person, who worked indefatigably for the community: Asma'u gave credibility to her accomplishments, noting:

She was a fine person who benefitted the Muslim Community.
She gave religious instruction to the ignorant and helped
everyone in their daily affairs.
Whenever called upon to help, she came, responding, to
lay out the dead without hesitation.
With the same willingness she attended women in
childbirth
All kinds of good works were performed by Zaharatu.
She was pious and most deserving: she delighted in giving
and was patient and forbearing. (vv. 6–10)

It may well be that when more documents come to light, elegies
will be found that were written by "princes" in praise of pious
barbers who circumcised boys, or bone setters who tended broken
limbs. However, it remains true to say that literature of this kind is
rare.

Hawa'u was a *jaji*, or leader of the bands of women students
known as *'yan-taru*, or "those who congregate together, the sisterhood." Asma'u relied on each *jaji* to act as a mentor and to bring
groups of women to her. To each she gave a large *malfa* hat made of
fine silky grasses. Usually worn by men, the hats have a distinctive
balloon shape because they are intended to be worn over turbans.
The late *Waziri* of Sokoto always wore one on formal public occasions. A *malfa* was also (and remains) one of the marks of the office
used by the *Inna* of Gobir, the chief of women devotees of *bori*.
Asma'u deliberately took up the symbol, and by giving each *jaji* a
malfa, she at once devalued its uniqueness and transformed what it
stood for. From being symbolic of *bori*, it turned into an emblem of
Islam. Asma'u ceremonially bestowed a red "turban,"[14] or strip of
red cloth, on each new appointee. Tied round the brim of the hat,
the turban was further proof of the wearer's authority and may have
been ceremoniously wrapped round the hat by Asma'u herself.

When students reached Asma'u, they went to her apartments
and were given refreshments. She talked to the older women, who
relayed to her the problems sent by the women left at home.
Through listening to her they learned how to apply the law and
make commonsense assessments. She received the young girls too,
smoothing her hands over their heads and praying that they would

marry good husbands and bring up their children in the Faith. By passing her hands over their heads a special kind of transfer of blessing-power was effected.

She became very attached to her devoted *jaji*s, especially the subject of this poem, Hawa'u. This elegy is more a remembrance of what Hawa'u represented than of the individual:

> I accept what has happened and remember Hawa'u who loved me, a fact well known to everybody.
> During the hot season, the rains, the harvest, when the harmattan blows and the beginning of the rains, she was on the road bringing people to me.
> She warned them to journey in good faith, for she said intention was important.
> As for myself, I taught them the religion of God in order to turn them from error, and instill in them the knowledge of their obligatory duties
> Like ritual ablution, prayer, alms, pilgrimage and the fast, all of which are compulsory for adults.
> I taught them what, in the Faith of Islam, is permissible and what is forbidden so they would know how to act.
> I said they must distance themselves from sins such as lying, meanness, hatred and envy,
> Adultery, theft and self-esteem. I said they should repent because these things lead to perdition.
> The women students and their children are well known for their good works and peaceful behavior in the community. (vv. 5–13)

It is clear that the educational network of which Hawa'u was a major part was central to the success and unity of the community. Thus, Hawa'u represents the generic woman, whose intellect and active promotion of education hold the community together.

Asma'u was not isolated, nor was she ever a lone voice. When she wrote, she addressed her contemporaries about shared problems. In addition, her works demonstrate how she went about organizing, educating, and reconciling the women of the Caliphate. To help her she had the relatives and friends with whom she had grown up and the activists she had recruited.

Contrary to what many imagine to be the case, educated women did not "enter purdah," disappearing into subordinate anonymity, when the new Islamic state was established. In the Caliphate there existed a world of women's Islam whose leaders held prestigious and powerful positions in the hierarchy of the Caliphate, a world which Asma'u's works reveal. It was well organized and efficiently run; it had clear objectives and a wide membership; it recruited from all ethnic groups and all age levels. Its political objectives were the conversion of women to Islam, education within Islam, and the harnessing of their talents to the development of the state. The potency and power of the *'yan-taru* movement has been borne out by its continued existence to the present day.

All this contradicts the views of those who have talked of "the men being Muslims and the women pagans"[15] or women being "on the periphery of the periphery of the Muslim world,"[16] or women silently subverting "the Islamic rules which keep them in an inferior position."[17] Such perspectives have contributed to negative stereotypes about Muslim women, in which they are depicted as different from active, independent African women of other ethnic, sociopolitical groups solely because of religious constraints. Those views derive from a paucity of women's voices in recorded history. The corpus of Asma'u's works can redress this situation, providing firsthand testimony to the active, necessary participation of women in Caliphate society.

Poems by Nana Asma'u

Appendix Those seeking more information about these poems
should consult *The Collected Works of Nana Asma'u,
1793–1864* by Jean Boyd and Beverly Mack, published by Michigan State University Press (1997).
Poems are presented here in the order in which they
appear in this volume.

ELEGY FOR BELLO

Sonnore Bello/Marthiya Bello

A.D. 1837/A.H. 1253

LANGUAGE OF ORIGINAL: FULFULDE/ARABIC
SOURCE OF TEXT: WAZIRI JUNAIDU

1   I rely on God the Enthroned, the Pure, the Omnipotent,
    To help me to accept what He has inflicted on me.
    May He help in my loneliness. Only God
    Can ease this loneliness, for He is All-Powerful.
        God the Almighty can work all things.

2   I rely on the most excellent of mortals,
    I invoke peace upon him
    Whose benevolence is free from taint
    Also on his relatives and Companions may there fall
        The peace of him whose guidance illuminates our Path.

3   Calling on him, I weep and compose this poem
    Shedding tears for the passing of the caliph
    I seek to soothe my heart
    In this world of sadness and confusion
        I relive the loss of my *shaikh*.

4   I am alone, missing the eternal love, the companionship
    Of my brother, we were confidants,
    He was my mentor;
    I shall never have that again.
        I cannot tell all, but will explain some points.

5   Restless and agitated I turn again to God the Pure on whom
        I rely
    I weep over my prayer beads
    And when I try to sleep I toss and turn
    In grief as I remember Bello.
        May God reunite us with him.

6   Reunite me with him in the realms of Heaven,
    O God most Holy, Gracious, You can do this.
    My sins terrify me

But I still hope for Your mercy.
    For Your Generosity is limitless.
7 I am like a small chicken
Whose mother died, leaving him crying forlornly.
Or like someone abandoned in the wilderness,
Howling until his ears are closed forever.
    God alone can wipe away my grief.
8 I am like an abandoned infant,
Left piteous and vulnerable,
Like a mother and father he cared for me,
That is how I remember him.
    Only the grace of God can help me.
9 He helped me in every respect as far as my religion and my
      worldly affairs, everything,
God knows, and so do the people.
He was my teacher.
He helped all people with their affairs:
    He had concern for their welfare and he did things
      according to religion.
10 He was upright, exceedingly generous, patient:
He spread learning and explained matters.
He was wise. He could turn back prodigals
And used his wits to remedy any situation.
    O God help us, for You are merciful.
11 In his day he was unique in his status
Among scholars and non-scholars alike.
He assuaged people's griefs and fears,
He was a refuge, a haven
    In our time. Listen to what I say.
12 He had a fine character, he was merciful to the poor, he
      honored
And befriended people.
He was gracious to strangers and generous to them,
Looked after their interests, fed them.
    It was his nature to be very generous.
13 He was never ill-tempered, he was pleasant to everyone;
Only if the law was broken did he become angry.
In that case he was implacable and could not be appeased.

When he regained equanimity he was calm.
These were his characteristics from his boyhood.

14 O God bestow on him Your blessings,
Your mercy, and perfume him
In his grave with Your favors;
Light up his tomb; give him honor
For the honor of he who exceeds honor, I make my plea.

15 On the Day of Resurrection may he be saved
By the grace of the Prophet
And drink from the Pool,
And be taken to Paradise, the abode of the Prophet.
By the grace of Ahmad.

16 May he see the face of the Prophet, the Chosen One,
And may he be with those who see God's Majesty.
May he be united with his father and mother and all Muslims
Who have followed Muhammad's way.
In the name of the Prophet, our leader.

17 Let us pray that God will help us now that Bello is gone
And give victory to his successor.
May he have a long life
And defend religion, as Bello did.
In the name of the Prophet I make this plea.

18 My poem is completed. May God accept it.
I give thanks
And invoke blessings on the Prophet,
His Companions and the saints.
I ask for enlightenment through the Prophet.

19 Count on good news from the *hijra* of the Prophet
To Medina, the date is fixed.
Count and see, take care. Reflect.
You know where he went,
And remember "God is our helper." Here the poem is complete.

Bello's Character

Gikku Bello

A.D. 1838–39/A.H. 1254

LANGUAGE OF ORIGINAL: FULFULDE

SOURCE OF TEXT: WAZIRI JUNAIDU

1 I give thanks to the King of Heaven, the One God.
   I invoke blessings on the Prophet and set down my
      poem.
2 The Lord made Heaven and earth and created all things,
   sent prophets to enlighten mankind.
3 Believe in them for your own sake, learn from them and be
      saved,
   believe in and act upon their sayings.
4 I invoke blessings on the Prophet who brought the Book,
   the Qur'an:
   he brought the *hadith* to complete the enlightenment.
5 Muslim scholars have explained knowledge and used it,
   following in the footsteps of the Prophet.
6 It is my intention to set down Bello's characteristics
   and explain his ways.
7 For I wish to assuage my loneliness, requite my love,
   find peace of mind through my religion.
8 These are his characteristics: he was learned in all branches
      of knowledge
   and feared God in public and in private.
9 He obeyed religious injunctions and distanced himself from
      forbidden things:
   this is what is known about him.
10 He concentrated on understanding what is right to know
   about the Oneness of God.
11 He preached to people and instructed them about God:
   he caused them to long for Paradise.
12 He set an example in his focus on eternal values:
   he strove to end oppression and sin.

13 He upheld the *shari'a*, honored it, implemented it aright,
    that was his way, everyone knows.

14 And he made his views known to those who visited him:
    he said to them "Follow the *shari'a*, which is sacred."

15 He eschewed worldly things and discriminated against
    anything of ill repute;
    he was modest and a repository of useful knowledge.

16 He was exceedingly level-headed and generous, he enjoyed
    periods of quietude:
    but was energetic when he put his hand to things.

17 He was thoughtful, calm, a confident statesman, and
    quick-witted.

18 He honored people's status: he could sort out difficulties
    and advise those who sought his help.

19 He had nothing to do with worldly concerns, but tried to
    restore to a healthy state
    things which he could. These were his characteristics.

20 He never broke promises, but faithfully kept them:
    he sought out righteous things. Ask and you will hear.

21 He divorced himself entirely from bribery and was totally
    scrupulous:
    He flung back at the givers money offered for titles.

22 One day Garange [chief of Mafora] sent him a splendid gift,
    but Bello told the messenger Zitaro to take it back.

23 He said to the envoy who had brought the bribe,
    "Have nothing to do with forbidden things."

24 And furthermore he said, "Tell him that the gift was sent for
    unlawful purposes;
    it is wrong to respond to evil intent."

25 He was able to expedite matters: he facilitated learning,
    commerce,
    and defense, and encouraged everything good.

26 He propagated good relationships between different tribes
    and between kinsmen. He afforded protection; everyone
    knows this.

27 When strangers came he met them, and taught about
    religious matters,
    explaining things: he tried to enlighten them.

28 He lived in a state of preparedness, he had his affairs in
      order
      and had an excellent intelligence service.

29 He had nothing to do with double agents and said it was
      better to ignore them,
      for they pervert Islamic principles.

30 He was a very pleasant companion to friends and acquain-
      tances:
      he was intelligent, with a lively mind.

31 He fulfilled promises and took care of affairs, but he did not
      act hastily.

32 He shouldered responsibilities and patiently endured adver-
      sities.

33 He was watchful and capable of restoring to good order
      matters which had gone wrong.

34 He was resourceful and could undo mischief, no matter how
      serious,
      because he was a man of ideas.

35 He was gracious to important people and was hospitable to
      all visitors,
      including non-Muslims.

36 He drew good people close to him and
      distanced himself from people of ill repute.

37 Those are his characteristics. I have recounted a few ex-
      amples
      that are sufficient to provide a model for emulation and
        benefit.

38 May God forgive him and have mercy on him:
      May we be united with him in Paradise, the place we
        aspire to.

39 For the sake of the Prophet, the Compassionate,
      who was sent with mercy to mankind.

40 May God pour blessings on the Prophet and
      his kinsmen and all other followers.

41 May God accept this poem. I have concluded it in the year
      1254.

The Qur'an

Sunago/Wa'kar Fadanci da Surorin Alkur'ani/Qasida fi'l Munaja

A.D. 1830/A.H. 1236: A.D. 1838/A.H. 1254: A.D. 1850/A.H. 1267 (?)

DATES: 1829–30 (FULFULDE), 1838–39 (HAUSA), 1850 (?) (ARABIC)

LANGUAGES: FULFULDE, HAUSA, ARABIC

SOURCES: FULFULDE, WAZIRI JUNAIDU; HAUSA, BAYERO
UNIVERSITY, KANO; ARABIC, MALAM BOYI OF KOFAR ATIKU

The Qur'an

1 I pray to God the Glorious
  Through the honor of Alhamdu and the *sura* Baƙara

2 And Ali Imarana and Nisa'u and Ma'idatu,
  Lan'ami, La'arafi and Lanfali and Bara

3 Through the honor of Yunusa, and Hudu, Yusufu, all,
  And the Ra'adu *sura*, Ibrahima and Hujura

4 And the *sura* of Nahali and Subuhana, so also Kahafi,
  Kahe and 'Dahe through their honor

5 With Anbiya'u, Hajji, Muminina and
  The *sura* of Nuri, also Furƙanu, and Shu'ara,

6 And Namli, 'Dasin, Ankabuti and
  The *sura* Rumu and Luƙumanu.

7 Raiba, Lahazabu, and Saba'in and Fa'diri
  Yasin and Saffi and Sadda and the *sura* Zumara

8 Gafiruz, Fussila and
  Shure and Zuhurufi and Duhanu.

9 Through the honor of Jasiya, Lahaƙafu include also
  Kitalu, Fatahu, also the *sura* Hujura,

10 And Kaf, Zari, and 'Duri I seek,
  Also Najami, and the *sura* Kamara,

11 Rahamanu, Waƙi'a, and Hadidi, Sami'a,
  For them all I pray and also the *sura* Hashara,

12 And Imtihanu, and Saffu, and the *sura* Jumu'a
  Munafiƙuna, Tagabuni, I believe in them all.

13 'Dalaƙu, Taharimu, Mulku and Nun I hope for,
  And Haƙatun and Ma'ariji, Nuhu,

14 And Jinnu, Mu'zzammilu, and Muddassiru also,
  Kiyama and the *sura* Insani.

15 And Mursalati and Naba'in and also
   waal-Nazi, A'ama, and Takawiri, Infadara,
16 Mudaffifina, and the *sura* Linshikaki also,
   Buruji, Dariki and Sabbi
17 With the blessings of Gashiya, Fajari,
   With the *sura* Baladi and Shamsi
18 Laili and Luhe and also Alam-nasharah
   I seek their refuge and Tini, Ikira
19 And the *sura* Kadari, Lam yaku and also
   Zilzila and Adiyati, I cite them all.
20 Through the blessings of Kari'a, Alheku and Asari,
   "Woe to those who . . .": "Haven't you seen . . ."
21 "The members of the tribe . . . ," "Have you seen . . ."
   And *Kausara*, Kafiruna and the *sura* Nasara
22 Be certain of Kulhuwa, and Kul a'uzu, and Zilfalaki
   So I have completed with Birabbinasi
23 God Almighty pour down blessings upon
   His Prophet who is our salvation on the day of judgment.
24 We are enlightened through the Qur'an, we are prepared
   Through his blessings; we will be ready.
25 I have finished the poem of the verses of the Qur'an;
   Through their sacredness I appeal to God.
26 Forgive my sins and give me
   Repentance and let me follow the *Sunna*, which protects me.
27 Protect me from earthly misfortunes and
   Also those of the grave, my Lord, and on the Last Day.
28 Forgive my mother and father,
   And all Muslims, I pray, Oh Powerful.
29 We thank God, we praise
   The Leader of mankind, we also pray for victory.
30 We ask for blessings on his Family and Companions
   And the followers of the *Sunna*, and those who thank God.

MEDICINE OF THE PROPHET

Tibb al-Nabi

A.D. 1839/A.H. 1255

LANGUAGE OF ORIGINAL: ARABIC

SOURCE OF TEXT: WAZIRI JUNAIDU

Introduction

In the name of God, the Beneficent, the Merciful. God bless and protect the noble Prophet, and his family, Companions, and sincere supporters.

Asma, daughter of the Shehu, the Commander of the Faithful, the light of the age, 'Uthman b. Fudi (may God be pleased with him and pour blessings upon him), said:

Now we proceed. This is a book which we have named "Glad tidings to Brethren on using the *suras* from the Qur'an of the generous Creator." God is the one who leads us in the right direction and unto Him we return. Success is due to God.

We begin with the *shahada* because it is the key to all good things.

The Exalted One said, "And he accepts his declaration"—namely, the statement "There is no god except God." It was related by the Messenger of God (may God bless and protect him), that four thousand grave sins will be wiped from the record of anyone who says, "There is no god except God" and prolongs it. Authenticated by *Kitab al-Zakki*.

It was also reported about him (may God bless and protect him), that he said, "Frequently say: 'There is no god except God.' I have never uttered any statement more important to the Lord of the Worlds, whether during life or near death, than 'There is no god except God.' Nor have angels close to God, prophets, messengers, pious worshipers, and those who praise the Lord of the Worlds uttered anything more important."

Whenever he entered the graveyard, he used to say: "Peace be upon the people who say 'There is no god except God.' How are the people who say, 'There is no god except God'? O God, by virtue of the statement 'There is no god except God,' forgive the people who say this phrase, and assemble us in their company." Authenticated by the *Risalah* of al-Qushayri.

He (may God bless and protect him) said: "God, glorious and sublime, says, 'By my glory and majesty, I will put no one who says there is no god but God in the fire.'"

He (may God bless and protect him) said: "No worshiper says simply and sincerely, 'There is no god but God' without the gates of Heaven being opened to him so as to lead him to the throne." He used to say also: "Faith has more than seventy branches, the lowest of which is the removal of injury from the path and the highest of which is to utter 'There is no god except God and Muhammad is his Prophet'" (may God bless and protect him). May God grant us the right to die while uttering this statement and may He make it easy for us to reach all these branches on account of the grace of Muhammad, may God bless and protect him.

He (may God bless and protect him) said: "I continued to plead for intercession and God continued to intercede for me until I asked, 'What about the person who says there is no god except God?' He replied, 'O Muhammad, that is not for you but for me to judge. By my glory and majesty, I will put no one who says there is no god except God in the fire.'"

He (may God bless and protect him) said: "God, glorious and majestic, says to the angels, 'Bring the people who say there is no god except God close to me, for I do love them.'"

He (may God bless and protect him) said: "Renew your faith." Then he was asked, "O messenger of God, how do we renew our faith?" He replied, "Say frequently, 'There is no god except God.'" Authenticated by the book of al-Qushayri.

The same thing applies to praying frequently for the Prophet (may God bless and protect him). This is because God and the angels bless the Prophet.

The Messenger of God (may God bless and protect him), said to his companions, "God has enriched me with your prayers but in fact God, majestic and glorious, has ordered you to do this as a generous gesture toward you."

He (may God bless and protect him) said: "Praying for me is a light in the heart, a lamp in the grave and a lantern on the path."

When light enters the heart, darkness departs from it and it is guided aright. No matter how difficult it may be to fulfill a desire, you must frequently bless him for he is the mediator between us and our Exalted Lord, and he is our guide to Him. From him emanates all of creation, from the prophets to the saints, and all of their works are presented to him (may God bless and protect him). By blessing him, light appears; and darkness does not cease except by the advent of light. Darkness refers to the filth which attaches itself to the soul, and the grime which clings to the heart. If the soul is purified of filth and the heart of grime, then all defects which stand in the way of goodness cease to be. It is not possible to imitate his deeds except by loving him to the utmost and that is not possible except by frequently praying for him. Whoever loves something constantly talks about it.

He (may God bless and protect him) said: "Every prayer is barred from God until it includes blessings upon Muhammad and the family of Muhammad." Related by al-Tabari in *al-Awsat*.

It is now time for us to mention some of the benefits of the *sura*s of the Qur'an.

Benefits of the Suras of the Qur'an

Surat al-Dukhan, Sura 44

Among the benefits of the *sura*s of the Qur'an is one which was related by Abu Hurayra (may God be pleased with him); [he said that] the Messenger of God (may God bless and protect him) said: "Whoever reads *Surat al-Dukhan* at night will have seventy thousand angels supplicate to God on his behalf for forgiveness and he will get up in the morning a forgiven man."

He (may God bless and protect him) said: "*Al-Dukhan* is invoked in the blessed realm of God. God and the angels bless the one who reads it."

He (may God bless and protect him) also said: "Whoever reads it on a Friday night is forgiven. God will build a house in Paradise for the one who reads it on a Friday."

He (may God bless and protect him) again said: "Whoever reads *Ya'sin* and *Dukhan* on Friday night, faithfully and in anticipation of God's reward, will have all his former sins forgiven. Whoever copies it and keeps the copy of it with him will be safe from every king and satan, and he will be feared and loved by everyone who meets him. If he drinks its water, it will be useful against dysentery and it will ease constipation." Authenticated by *Manafi' al-Qur'an*.

Surat ul-Qital, Sura 47

Among its benefits is one which he (may God bless and protect him) stated: "God will oblige the one who reads *Surat ul-Qital* by granting him a drink from the rivers of Paradise."

Surat ul-Fath, Sura 48

Among its benefits is one which the messenger of God (may God bless and protect him) stated: "Whoever recites *Surat ul-Fath* on the first night in the month of Ramadan, or voluntarily on the first night of the month of Ramadan, will be protected during the year."

It was related by one of the *Salihin* [pious men] that whoever reads it three times when he sees the crescent moon on the first night of Ramadan will have God increase his income until the end of that year.

Surat al-Najm, Sura 53

He (may God bless and protect him) said: "Whoever reads *Surat al-Najm* will be given the reward for ten good deeds multiplied by the number of those who believed in Muhammad (may God bless and protect him), and multiplied by the number of those who did not."

Whoever writes it on a clean piece of gazelle-leather and wears it will increase his power and will defeat anyone who disputes him, for it will become to him a source of strength and support. Authenticated by *Manafi' al-Qur'an*.

Surat al-Qamar, Sura 54

He (may God bless and protect him) said: "Whoever writes *Surat al-Qamar* on a Friday and wears it on himself or under his turban will become an eminent man among his people. Difficult matters will become easy for him with God's permission."

He (may God bless and protect him) said: "In the realm of God, this *sura* is called 'the whitener which whitens the face of its reciter on the day when some faces shall be bright and others gloomy.'" Authenticated from *Manafi' al-Qur'an*.

Surat al-Rahman, Sura 55

He (may God bless and protect him) said: "Recite *Surat al-Rahman*, praise God twice, and give thanks for what God has bestowed on you. And if you see a dog growling, say, 'O ye jinns and men: if you have the power to pass into the regions of the heavens and the earth, then do so; but you will not penetrate into them except by my authority.'"

It was reported by him (may God bless and protect him): "The reader of *al-Rahman* and *al-Waqi'a* and *al-Hadid* is called in the realm of Heaven 'a Paradise dweller.'" Authenticated from *Manafi' al-Qur'an*.

Surat al-Waqi'a, Sura 56

'Abd Allah ibn Mas'ud (may God be pleased with him) said: "I heard the Messenger of God (may God bless and protect him) say: 'Whoever reads *Surat al-Waqi'ah* every night will never be stricken by poverty and whoever reads it early every morning will never fear impoverishment.'"

One of the *Salihin* [pious men] said: "If it is read for a dead person, he will be relieved of his sins; if read for a sick person, he will be made comfortable. If written and worn by a woman undergoing childbirth, she will safely deliver the child by the grace of God the Exalted One. It is effective on everything to which it is attached."

He said: "Whoever copies it and reads it frequently in the morning and at night while in a ritually clean state will neither be hungry nor thirsty; even if he reads it only once no hardship, fear, or poverty will befall him. Whoever feels pain in the liver and wears a copy of it will recover. Its benefits are great and its reward is enormous." Authenticated from *Manafi' al-Qur'an*.

Surat al-Mujadala, Sura 58

He (may God bless and protect him) said: "Whoever reads *Surat al-Mujadala* will be placed under the protection of God the

Exalted One on the Day of Judgment. If it is read for a sick person, that person will sleep peacefully. Whoever continues to read it night and day will be preserved from every calamity. If it is read for an item which is stored somewhere else, it will be safe until it is taken out of that place. If it is written down and thrown into stored grain, it will remove anything that can spoil it." This was authenticated; see *Manafi' al-Qur'an*.

Surat al-Hashr, Sura 59

There is nothing in existence—neither paradise, hellfire, the throne of majesty, the seat of divine authority, the mystic veil, the seven firmaments and seven earths, the wind, birds, trees, creeping animals, mountains, the sun, the moon, nor angels—that will not pray for and seek forgiveness on behalf of anyone who reads *Surat al-Hashr*. If he who read it should die on that very day, then he will die a martyr.

Hujjat al-Islam Abu Hamid Muhammad al-Ghazali (may God be pleased with him) said: "Whoever reads *al-Hashr* is protected in his religious and temporal life."

Some experts say that the end of *al-Hashr* is a remedy for every form of sickness except death itself. This is authenticated from *Manafi' al-Qur'an*.

Surat al-Juma'a, Sura 62

It was reported by the Prophet (may God bless and protect him): "Whoever reads *Surat al-Juma'a* will be granted forgiveness for sins up to the number of those who attend the Friday congregational prayer. Anyone who persists in reading it shall be safe from the whispers of Satan and shall be forgiven for everything he did on that particular night." According to the statement of God the Exalted One: "That is the grace of God which He grants to whomever He wishes. The grace of God is great." Whoever engraves this verse on a shell and throws it into his coffers will be blessed, and will be protected from all harm. Authenticated from *Madarik*.

Surat al-Mulk, Sura 67

He (may God bless and protect him) said: "One *sura* of the Qur'an which has thirty verses shall act on behalf of a man until

he is forgiven for his sins, and that *sura* is *Suratu Tabaraka 'lladhi.*"
It was reported by Ibn Mas'ud (may God be pleased with him):
"Learn *Surat al-Mulk* for it prevents one from suffering in the tomb
and from Munkar and Nakir, and it eases the onset of death."

Surat al-Qalam, Sura 68

He (may God bless and protect him) said: "To whoever reads
Suratu Nun wa-al-Qalam God will grant the reward of those whose
conduct was good. And if it is copied down and hung on someone
whose teeth hurt, then his pain will subside by permission of God,
the Exalted One." Authenticated from *Manafi' al-Qur'an.*

Surat al-Haqqa, Sura 69

He (may God bless and protect him) said: "Whoever reads
Surat al-Haqqa will be judged leniently by God. If it is worn by a
pregnant woman, then she will be protected from all ailments."

Surat al-Ma'arij, Sura 70

It was related by the Prophet (may God bless and protect him)
that: "To whoever reads *Surat al-Ma'arij*, God will give the reward
of 'those who are trustworthy and honor their pledge' and 'those
who are constant in their prayer.' Whoever reads it at night will be
safe from ritual impurity and from bad dreams and frightening
visions."

Surat Nuh, Sura 71

It was related by Ubayy ibn Ka'b (may God be pleased with
him) that the Prophet (may God bless and protect him) said:
"Whoever reads *Surat al-Nuh* will be counted among the believers
who benefitted from the prayer of Noah (peace be upon him).

Whoever perseveres in reading it will not die until he has seen
his place in Paradise. Whoever reads it and then seeks to fulfill one
of his needs will easily do so.

Whoever reads this *sura* will be rescued from his prison. If he is
sad and depressed, his sadness and depression will cease. Whoever
reads it on a journey will travel smoothly and will be safe from
enemies. Whoever reads it when in debt will have his debt offset by
God; whoever reads it when destitute will have his hardship end.

Whoever meets a tyrant will be safe from his wickedness and his needs will be seen to." Authenticated from *Manafi' al-Qur'an*.

Surat al-Jinn, Sura 72

It was related by the Prophet (may God bless and protect him): "Whoever reads *Surat al-Jinn* and then frees a slave will be rewarded according to the number of jinns who believed Muhammad (may God bless and protect him) and the number of jinns who did not believe him (may God bless and protect him).

If it is read somewhere, then the demons there will be disturbed by its reading. If a captive reads it, then God will open the door of escape for him and he will be protected until he returns to his people.

Whoever reads it on his way to the ruler will be safeguarded from the ruler's tyranny. If it is read on behalf of something which is stored away, it will be preserved by the grace of God. If it is read by someone who is locked up, his escape will be made easy." Authenticated from *Manafi' al-Qur'an*.

Surat al-Muzammal, Sura 73

It was related by the Prophet (may God bless and protect him) that whoever reads *Surat al-Muzammal* will be protected from any distressful situation in this world and in the Hereafter. Anyone who persists in reading it will see the Prophet (may God bless and protect him) and can ask of him anything he wishes.

Surat al-Qiyama, Sura 75

It was related by the Prophet (may God bless and protect him): "Whoever reads *Surat al-Qiyama* will be resurrected with a glowing face. By reading it, hearts are humbled and are endowed with security and affection. Anyone who reads it will have no fear of demons. If one reads it in the daytime, one will be protected throughout the night and vice versa.

Whoever wants to fill his heart with humility and fear of his Lord, let him read it. Anyone who does read it will be protected from rulers and tyrants. Whoever reads it at night will be protected from evil spirits and demons." Authenticated from *Manafi' al-Qur'an*.

Suratu Hal Ata 'ala al-Insan, Sura 76

It was related by Abu Ubayy ibn Ka'b (may God be pleased with him) that "whoever reads *Suratu Hal Ata 'ala al-Insan* will have a reward of Paradise and silk from God.

Whoever reads it will have peace of mind and heart. And if he is unable to read it, then he should have it copied, rub it off into water, and drink it.

Whoever persists in reading it will have self-confidence, and words of wisdom will emanate from his mouth." Authenticated from *Manafi' al-Qur'an.*

Surat al-Mursalat, Sura 77

The messenger of God (may God bless and protect him) said: "Whoever reads *Surat al-Mursalat* will be free from polytheism. If it is written on a new earthenware utensil which is then ground up, sieved, and drunk with rainwater by a sick person, the person will get well.

Whoever hangs it on someone who has boils will cause the boils to vanish. Whoever is in litigation will have mastery over and will be stronger than the one suing him.

Whoever copies it and wears it will have a stronger argument, so that he can defeat his enemy and subdue his adversary.

If someone who breaks out in pimples and boils writes it on a piece of paper and attaches it to himself, then he will be cured of them." Authenticated from *Manafi' al-Qur'an.*

Suratu 'amma yatasa'alun, Sura 78

The Messenger of God (may God bless and protect him) said: "Anyone who reads *Suratu 'amma yatasa'alun* will be given a cold drink by God on Resurrection Day. Anyone who reads it because he wants to stay awake all night will be able to stay awake all night."

If you read it for someone who is traveling at night, it will guard him from every nighttime marauder and protect him from all harmful things.

Whoever ties a copy of it to his forearm and goes with it to see a ruler whom he dreads will be safe from the ruler's evil.

Surat al-Nazi'at, Sura 79

It was related by the Prophet (may God bless and protect him): "The sultan will honor and satisfy the needs of whomever reads *Surat al-Nazi'at* while entering his presence. He will also be protected from his injustice.

And whoever reads it while receiving the enemy will be protected from his mischief and he will pay him no heed.

And whoever reads it in a frightening situation will not be affected by his fear of that place."

Surat 'Abasa, Sura 80

It was related by the Prophet (may God bless and protect him): "Whoever reads *Suratu 'Abasa* will come forth on the Day of Resurrection with a smiling, cheerful face.

Whoever writes it on a piece of paper and carries it with him will see nothing except good things on any path that he follows and will be guarded from any negative consequences of his route."

Surat al-Takwir, Sura 81

He (may God bless and protect him) said: "When God spreads out His scroll, He will prevent anyone who reads *Surat al-Takwir* from being disgraced. Let he who enjoys the anticipation of Resurrection Day read it too. Whoever reads it when rain is falling will be granted forgiveness according to the total number of raindrops that fall. Whoever reads it in a house where a buried charm cannot be located will be inspired to find it by God the Exalted One; no harm will befall him and its spell will be rendered ineffective on the one for whom it was intended.

Whoever reads it for an ailing eye will have the eye's vision sharpened, and its swelling and discharge will cease." Authenticated from *Madarik*.

Surat al-Mutaffifin, Sura 83

He (may God bless and protect him) said: "To whoever reads *Surat al-Mutaffifin*, God will offer the sealed nectar. If it is read for something which is stored away, it will protect that item against damage by insects."

Surat al-Buruj, Sura 85

It was related by the Prophet (may God bless and protect him): "Whoever reads *Surat al-Buruj* will be given the reward of one who stands on 'Arafat. Its special characteristic: when hung on a weaned child, it makes the weaning process easier to bear.

Anyone who reads it while on his bed will be under God's protection until the next morning."

God encompasses them from behind [unexpectedly]. "If you read this verse at the door of your house three times when you want to travel, then the house and everything in it—including the people, property, and money—will be protected from all calamities. If it is read for a child, he will be guarded from all harmful things." Authenticated from *Manafi' al-Qur'an.*

Surat al-Tariq, Sura 86

God will guard anyone who reads *Surat al-Tariq* from his enemy, and He will shield him from his adversaries. He will also credit him with ten good deeds for every star in the sky.

Its special property: If it is read over a medicine to be ingested, then a person will be made safe from any side effect and it will be effective by the grace of God. And if someone cleans a wound with its water, the wound will not re-open. Whoever fears bad dreams should read it at bedtime as far as the words "he would have no power or might" so that he would not have nightmares.

Suratu Sabbih Isma Rabbika al-A'la, Sura 87

It was related by the Prophet (may God bless and protect him): "Whoever reads *Suratu Sabbih Isma Rabbika al-A'la* when he wakes up will earn the rewards of three pilgrimages."

He (may God bless and protect him) used to repeat: "Praise the names of God the Most High," "Say O disbelievers," and "Say, He is God, the only One," as well as the *Mu'awwidhatayn.*

Its special property: If read on behalf of a deaf ear, it will put an end to its deafness. If read for hemorrhoids, then they will go away. It is a source of protection against the evil eye and it is an effective antidote to any harm.

Surat al-Ghashiya, Sura 88

It was related by Ubayy ibn Ka'b (may God be pleased with him) that the Messenger of God (may God bless and protect him) said:

"Whoever reads *Surat al-Ghashiya* will be judged lightly by God on the Day of Judgment."

Its special property: Whoever reads it over anything to be eaten will be insured against any harm from the food. Whoever reads it for pain will be relieved.

Surat al-Fajr, Sura 89

Whoever reads *Surat al-Fajr* during the first ten nights of the month will be forgiven by God. It will be a light on Resurrection Day for whoever reads it on the other days of the month.

Whoever reads it at night on the eleventh day of the month will be free from fear until sunrise. Whoever reads it a hundred times during the night and then has sexual relations with his wife will be blessed with a boy who will be a delight to his heart.

Some say that the ten nights are the nights of Dhu al-Hijja, others say the first ten of Muharram, and still others claim the last ten of Ramadan. Authenticated from *Manafi' al-Qur'an*.

Suratu La Uqsimu bi-Hadha al-Balad, Sura 90

It was related by Ubayy ibn Ka'b (may God be pleased with him) regarding the Prophet (may God bless and protect him) that he said:

"Whoever reads *Suratu la Uqsimu bi-Hadha al-Balad* will be granted protection from God's anger on Resurrection Day."

Its special property: If hung on a child at birth, the child will be protected from any evils and from colic pain.

And if the child is made to take a sniff of its water, he will have sound nostrils, be free from colds, and grow up in good health.

Surat al-Shams, Sura 91

It was reported by the Prophet (may God bless and protect him): "Whoever reads *Surat al-Shams wa Duhaha* will be free from any fear."

Surat al-Layl, Sura 92

It was reported by Ubayy ibn Ka'b (may God be pleased with him) that the Prophet of God (may God bless and protect him) said:

"God will reward whoever reads *Suratu wa al-Layl Idha Yaghsha* until he is satisfied. He will safeguard him from poverty, make life easy for him, protect him from evil, and grant him contentment, acceptance, and security."

Its special property: Whoever reads it once on the night of the fifteenth day of the month will see no hateful things in his dreams and will sleep peacefully.

It can be read into the ears of an unconscious person or an epileptic.

It is beneficial to someone who has a chronic fever. If he drinks its water, he will be cured by permission of God the Exalted One.

Surat al-Duha, Sura 93

He (may God bless and protect him) said:

"Whoever reads *Surat al-Duha* will earn the same reward as someone who visits Mina and 'Arafat. If it is read over the name of one who has been away for a long time, he will return home. If it is recited in regard to an object whose owner has forgotten its location, then the owner will remember it. Similarly, whoever forgets something and continuously recites *Surat al-Duha* will recollect what he has forgotten. And whoever loses something and recites it seven times will, if God so wishes, find it."

Suratu Iqra' bi-Ism Rabbika, Sura 96

It was reported by Abu Hurayra that the Prophet (may God bless and protect him) said:

"For whoever reads *Surat Iqra bi-Ism Rabbika*, it is as if he read *al-Mufassal*. What God has prepared for him in Paradise is beyond what any writer has ever described."

Its special property: Whoever reads it while setting out on a journey will be protected against any evil until he returns to his family, by permission of God. He will be safe from the dangers of water and from the fear of water.

Surat al-Qadr, Sura 97

He (may God bless and protect him) said:

"Whoever reads *Surat al-Qadr* one hundred times will have God put the most important of His names into his head so that he can pray for whatever he desires and have his needs fulfilled.

Whoever reads it one thousand times on a Friday will not die until he sees Muhammad (may God bless and protect him) in his sleep."

He said: "Do you wish that God would place a dam like that of Ya'juj and Ma'juj between you and the Devil?" They said: "Yes." He said: "Recite: 'We revealed it on Laylat al-Qadr' until the end, three times after the sunset prayer and the daybreak prayer but before you stand up. Then you should say: 'O Almighty God, relieve me of all my griefs and anxieties.'"

Surat Lam Yakun, Sura 98

The Prophet (may God bless and protect him) said regarding it: "If the people were to realize the importance of *Surat Lam Yakun*, then they would offer up their family and their wealth in order to learn it, and no hypocrite or doubting worshiper would read it. And as soon as a worshiper finished reciting it at night, God would send angels to protect him in his religious and worldly affairs and they would pray on his behalf for forgiveness and mercy. If he recited it in the daytime, he would receive as a reward the equivalent of daytime's illumination and nighttime's darkness combined."

Surat Idha Zulzilat, Sura 99

The Messenger of God (may God bless and protect him) said:

"*Surat Idha Zulzilat* is equal to half of the Qur'an. Say: 'He is God, the only One'; that is equal to one-third of the Qur'an.

And say: 'O you Unbelievers'; that is equal to one-fourth of the Qur'an.

Whoever constantly recites *Suratu Idha Zulzilat* in most of his prayers will have one of the treasures of this world and of the Hereafter opened up to him and in place of that he will be given an exalted position in Paradise."

Surat al-'Adiyat, Sura 100

He (may God bless and protect him) said: "For whoever reads *Surat al-'Adiyat*, it will be as if he has read half of the Qur'an."

Its special property: Whoever copies it and carries it on his person will be free from whatever may be frightening him.

God will make it easy for whoever recites it to obtain his sustenance. His fears and anxieties will be allayed, and his hunger and thirst will cease. And if someone who is burdened with debt recites it, then God the Exalted One will relieve him of that debt.

Surat al-Qari'a, Sura 101

Its merit:

He (may God bless and protect him) said: "On Resurrection Day, God the Exalted One will weigh the scales in favor of whoever reads *Surat al-Qari'a*."

Its special property: If worn by someone who is out of work and whose source of sustenance is uncertain, it will benefit him. And whoever reads it will come under God's shelter.

Surat al-Hakun al-Takathur, Sura 102

It was reported by Asma' bint 'Amis that the Prophet of God (may God bless and protect him) said:

"God will pardon whoever reads *Surat al-Hakun al-Takathur*, and He will not call him to account for his sins due to the favors which He has bestowed upon him in this world."

Its special property: If read following the afternoon prayer it will be effective against headaches and migraines, by God's permission.

Whoever reads it while rain is falling will earn God's forgiveness. Whoever reads it during the afternoon prayer and at sunset will come under God's protection until sunset the following day.

Surat al-'Asr, Sura 103

He (may God bless and protect him) said:

"God will put a seal of patience on whomever reads *Surat al-'Asr*, and he will be reckoned among those whose claim to reward is recognized on the Day of Judgment."

Its special property: If read on something before it is hidden, it will be safe from any interference. Whoever recites it seven times while rain is falling will earn for himself an inestimable treasure.

Surat al-Humaza, Sura 104

He (may God bless and protect him) said:
"Whoever reads *Surat al-Humaza* will not be the subject of ridicule. If it is read for someone who is afflicted by the evil eye, he will be cured by God's permission. Whoever recites it frequently during extra prayer sessions will have his wealth and sustenance increased."

Surat Li-'ilafi Quraysh, Sura 105

It was reported by Ubayy ibn Ka'b (may God be pleased with him) that the Messenger of God (may God bless and protect him) said: "Whoever reads *Surat Li-'ilafi Quraysh* will be secure from all frightening things."

Its special property: If recited over a piece of food, it will serve as a cure for all ailments. Shaykh Abu al-Hasan said: "As for *Surat Li-'Ilafi Quraysh*, whoever reads it is protected against indigestion, nausea, and pain."

Surat Ara'ayta, Sura 107

Whoever reads *Surat Ara'ayta* will be forgiven. Its special property: Anyone who reads it one hundred times after the evening prayer will be protected by God until daybreak.

Surat al-Kawthar, Sura 108

The Messenger of God (may God bless and protect him) said: "God will allow whoever reads *Surat Inna A'tainaka al-Kawthar* to drink from the rivers of Paradise."

Its special property: He who reads it at night one thousand times, then blesses the Prophet (may God bless and protect him) one thousand times, and then sleeps, will see the Prophet (may God bless and protect him) in his dreams.

And for anyone who copies it and wears it, it will serve as an amulet and a source of protection and support against enemies. No harmful thing will befall him as long as he wears it.

It was stated in *al-Mu'awwidhatayni* that nothing is as effective as this *sura* in seeking God's protection. Also, it was reported by Ibrahim ibn Adham that it was said to him: "Why do we pray without being answered?" He replied, "Because He called you and you failed to respond."

Then God the Exalted One said: "He grants the requests of those who believe and who do righteous deeds, and He supplies them with provisions from His abundance." That is, when they pray to him, he answers them and supplies them with more than they have requested.

Members of the community of the Prophet (may God bless and protect him) asked:

"Is our Lord close at hand so that we can whisper to Him, or far away so that we have to shout to Him?" Then it was revealed:

"I am close at hand to answer the entreaties of the supplicant if he beseeches Me, so let them heed Me and believe in Me, and perhaps they will be guided aright."

Ahmad Zarruq said in his *Qawa'id*: "The characteristics found in sayings, deeds, and precious things are unchanging. The greatest qualities of all are those of the *adhkar*, for there is no human deed more effective in escaping God's wrath than the recounting of the *dhikr* of God. God has placed *adhkar* in relation to the usefulness of all material things that concern Him, such as kneaded dough and liquids." And he goes on to say: "the natural yearning of the soul for wholesome things which have religious merit is legitimate." Hence the legitimacy of the desire for performing *adhkar* and *'ibadat* on behalf of worldly matters. This includes such things as the reading of *Surat al-Waqi'a* for warding off poverty; saying the *basmala*, which is an unfailing protection for anything on which it is invoked, both on earth and in heaven; saying, "He is all-hearing and all-knowing" for warding off sudden calamities; reciting, "I take refuge from the evil of His creatures in God's perfect words," for warding off injury from poisonous things and for protection in the home, and other such *adhkar*—for warding off sorrow and getting rid of debts, for achieving certain things such as wealth or safe travel and the like. An explanation for this is that if the *adhkar* achieve the desired result, then that would be a reason for liking them. In turn, that would lead to a love for the one who enabled this (and the one to whom their root and branches are traced) and this leads to the love of God.

If it does not bring about the desired result, it will nonetheless engender a feeling of graciousness, not less than that which the soul experiences by invocation of the True One. Entry into this state of grace is, naturally, possible and easy.

This is the principle on which Abu al-'Abbas al-Buni and others of his line of thought base their conclusions in connection with *dhikr al-asma'* and its special qualities. Otherwise, the principle would be that stated by our uncle, Shaikh 'Abdullah ibn Muhammad ibn Fudi (may God have mercy upon him) in his book *Diya' al-Qawa'id wa-Nathr al-Fawa'id li-ahl al-Maqasid*. Namely, "as a matter of respect, *al-adhkar* and *'ibadat* should not be used merely for attaining worldly objectives, though God knows best."

I composed my book in the fortress of my *Shaikh*
    The one called Bello, my bosom friend, my brother
Generous, he was proclaimed a caliph
    Heir to the Reformer, Shaikh of Shaikhs
O my soul, weep over our bereavement of him!
    I am, nonetheless, satisfied by the blessings from him
Praise be to my Lord who has bestowed upon me
    Abundant kindness and favors
May Allah compensate us for the loss of goodness
    On the honor of the Prophet and his sacredness
May the blessing of Allah and the purest peace
    Rest upon the best of mankind, and His Mercy,
Also on his descendants, his companions and following generation
    And followers of the followers of his *Sunna.*
In coded figures five and fifty years
    Plus one thousand and two hundred of the *Hijra,*
It was completed on Tuesday, three
    Days remaining in the month of Sha'ban toward its end.

BE SURE OF GOD'S TRUTH

Tabbat Hakika

A.D. 1831–32/A.H. 1247

LANGUAGE OF ORIGINAL: HAUSA
SOURCE OF TEXT: MALAM GARBA GERAU

1   Let us praise the King, *hakika*, in Truth
   Who is merciful and generous, *hakika*, in Truth
   Mankind is fully aware of this, *hakika*, in Truth
   Thanks be to God the Sovereign, *hakika*, in Truth
       One God sufficient for all, *Be sure of God's Truth.*

2   Kinsmen, let us pray ceaselessly for the Prophet
   With attention to detail let us beseech the Prophet
   That tomorrow we might find salvation through the Prophet
   Let us pray and invoke blessings on the Prophet
       Ahmadu who excelled all, *Be sure of God's Truth.*

3   Let everyone consider and reflect.
   I will give you good advice: be respected.
   Let us continue to follow the Path, and escape retribution
   Listen to my song and repent
       And so find salvation, *Be sure of God's Truth.*

4   Whether a man has a high position,
   Whether he is a ruler or a poor man,
   Whether he is powerful and miserly, or powerful and
       generous,
   Whoever fails to revere the Caliph
       Will die ignorant, *This is God's Truth.*

5   No matter how pious you are,
   Nor how godly and saintly,
   Nor how profoundly learned,
   All who refuse to follow the commands of the Caliph
       Will be without excuse Hereafter, *Be sure of God's Truth.*

6   As for you if you are the Caliph, you must act generously
   You are warned not to be mean

So you will be trusted by the people
He who is Caliph and acts righteously
Will be in Paradise Hereafter, *Be sure of God's Truth.*

7 If you become the Caliph, with authority over people
You are to look after the interests of everyone.
Strive hard to do well for fear you will burn.
He who becomes Caliph to devour the people
Will be consumed by fire Hereafter, *Be sure of God's Truth.*

8 Whoever seeks a position of authority
So that he can get rich or become powerful,
Or slyly allies himself with wrongdoers,
And those who pay money for titles of authority
Without doubt will burn Hereafter, *Be sure of God's Truth.*

9 Anyone who wants to find peace
In this world and the next should act peacefully,
And anyone who refuses my advice will be sorry.
But the lowest village chief who is merciful
Will escape Hereafter, *Be sure of God's Truth.*

10 Obey your leaders, listen to what they say
It is your religious duty regardless of their characters.
Whether they are good or bad, you must obey them:
Those who refuse because the rulers do not benefit them
Will burn Hereafter, *Be sure of God's Truth.*

11 Rulers must persevere to improve affairs,
Do you hear? And you who are ruled, do not stray:
Do not be too anxious to get what you want.
Those who oppress the people in the name of authority
Will be crushed in their graves Hereafter, *Be sure of God's Truth.*

12 Act righteously toward the people and do not cheat.
Be always compassionate toward them; your reward is in the Hereafter.
Do not follow those who have strayed from the Path
Those who prevent the victims from lodging complaints
Will themselves be kept from access to Heaven, *Be sure of God's Truth.*

13 Some have obeyed and resolutely keep the laws
   That God has made: they have joined our Jihad.
   Others have disobeyed, deliberately, and have flouted the
      laws
   They move about doing all kinds of evil
      They will roam in hellfire, *Be sure of God's Truth.*

14 Those with a case should seek legal redress
   Instead they choose to go to influential people.
   They do not seek lawful judgment, as instructed.
   Those who cause commotions and spread slander
      Will be shrieking in the Hereafter, *Be sure of God's Truth.*

15 If the judge summons you, you must go:
   To refuse the call is to disobey God.
   Go to the judge, and do not look elsewhere
   Anyone who refuses to answer the summons of a judge
      Will be summoned by the Fire, *Be sure of God's Truth.*

16 The angry person who is irate with the judge,
   Or is abusive, lacks respect.
   You are not to act like this even in jest,
   Nor refuse to accept the decisions
      That the judge makes, *Be sure of God's Truth.*

17 However, if the judge, in making his judgments
   Refuses to follow the Path, he is guilty of oppression
   In the Next World, he will be shackled,
   For if the judge changes the law
      He has become an infidel, *Be sure of God's Truth.*

18 Instruct your people to seek redress in the law
   Whether you are a minor official or the *Imam* himself.
   Even if you are learned, do not stop them,
   All those who prevent their people from pursuing the law
      Will go to the Fire, *Be sure of God's Truth.*

19 We have been warned, kinsmen, to be constantly obedient
   And at all times worthy of salvation.
   Do not therefore disregard the law in any respect.
   He who unravels legal judgments
      Will be flogged in the Hereafter, *Be sure of God's Truth.*

20 A person who breaks a promise is a cheat
   And he who treats his people contemptuously must repent

For he has sinned. Who is he like? See—
The enslaver of a freeman who inflicts on him harsh treat-
     ment—
     The Fire will enslave them all, *Be sure of God's Truth.*

21   There will be no escape, Hereafter, for witches
     Unless they quickly repent.
     There are others doing wrong, miscreants
     Those who grab land, and flaunt their gain,
          Will bear the burden of it Hereafter, *Be sure of God's
          Truth.*

22   There are those who inflate market prices:
     And others who double-deal when selling.
     There are still others, let me tell you
     Who swallow up the wealth of the treasury
          The Fire will swallow them, *Be sure of God's Truth.*

23   The same goes for the thieves in the villages
     And towns, who rob and take away.
     Those who strip a room and take its contents,
     And those who illegally conceal booty
          They will be revealed, *Be sure of God's Truth.*

24   If you join the Jihad, give heed—
     You fight for God's sake, do not forget.
     Those who cheat their companions using evil charms,
     And those who use brute force to wrest things illegally,
          Will be exposed, *Be sure of God's Truth.*

25   When a town is captured wreak no vengeance
     Wrongdoing is unworthy of us.
     Yet some of us are always defaulting:
     Those who steal booty from those who first captured it
          Will be seized by the Fire, *Be sure of God's Truth.*

26   Captured booty must definitely not be hidden:
     War trophies must be taken to the leader.
     There are those, without doubt, who conceal booty.
     Those who deny the poor their rightful share
          Will receive the Fire as their share, *Be sure of God's
          Truth.*

27   When the army is victorious
     Slaves are taken, including some for the leader

But some men act illegally
They fall on the women, disregarding all sanctions:
> They will fall in the Fire, *Be sure of God's Truth.*

28 Be fair in all your dealings, even about the smallest thing.
Do not dupe people headed to the market to sell.
It is wrong, like reclaiming gifts you have given away.
Those who are untrustworthy Hereafter
> Will have no trust left, *Be sure of God's Truth.*

29 You have been warned to practice no oppression
So that you will receive the pardon of God the Bountiful.
Anyone who refuses will eat the bitter fruit of Hell,
And he who robs with violence, including Muslims,
> Or breaks faith, will burn, *Be sure of God's Truth.*

30 Let us study, and keep on learning:
This gives mankind all that he needs.
Do not stay among ignorant people
Who violently seize property in Muslim lands.
> The Fire will seize them, *Be sure of God's Truth.*

31 Some waste their energy where the music is wild.
They find it impossible to return to the Path.
They refuse to reform.
Those who snatch and grab in the market
> Will be snatched by Fire, *Be sure of God's Truth.*

32 Ruthless and envious people will
Be taken to the Fire where it is red hot.
When they are put there, they immediately swell up,
Evil people, adulterers, and kidnappers,
> Will all go to the Fire, *Be sure of God's Truth.*

33 My warnings are uttered to wake you up
Always live in the fear of God, beseeching Him
This is the real truth, there is no mistake
Rulers who create mayhem when collecting alms
> Will themselves be caught, *Be sure of God's Truth.*

34 Those who in themselves are not erudite,
Are lost because they never ask even about the things
   essential
To knowing the Path. Let this not be so!
Those who lie with their wives at will and not in turn
> Will have their turn in the Fire, *Be sure of God's Truth.*

35 The person who does not repent truly will burn.
Listen to my admonition and take care.
Do not cover up for anyone, even relatives
He who refuses to sleep with his wives in turn
　　Will twist in hellfire, *Be sure of God's Truth.*

36 Some people's sole means of livelihood is in seizing property
　　by force:
Others lie waiting, concealed, in order to steal.
Others cheat: they are there in readiness.
Women who bind their husbands with spells
　　Will be bound up in Hell, *Be sure of God's Truth.*

37 Some will go to the Fire of Sa'ira,
Others to the Fire of Sijin, others to the Fire of Sakara.
All were disobedient and will go to the Fire of Naru,
Including women who go out unnecessarily,
　　They will not escape the Fire, *Be sure of God's Truth.*

38 Anyone who presses a poor man to repay a loan,
Or an excessively jealous woman,
Who has been warned that this is unseemly,
And any wife who uses a spell to hurt her co-wife
　　Will be humiliated tomorrow, *Be sure of God's Truth.*

39 Some commit many sins
And because of their evil deeds, they attract wrongdoers
Knaves, who gather from near and far,
Sorcerers and the makers of evil charms
　　Will go to hellfire, *Be sure of God's Truth.*

40 These warnings are intended to wake you up
To prepare you for the place you will go to in the Hereafter.
Stop rushing to people for favors
The persistent wheedler will find in the Hereafter, his face
　　Has been turned about, *Be sure of God's Truth.*

41 You are warned to do your best at all times
Be always merciful to your kinsmen and generous
Those who cheat colleagues intending to harm them
And those who disrupt family harmony
　　Are nothing but firewood to burn, *Be sure of God's Truth.*

42 Anyone who turns his energies toward oppression
And refuses to repent, and he who set his learning aside
Has reaped no benefit from his existence

Gossip mongers who divide the community
    Will see Paradise? Indeed not! *Be sure of God's Truth.*
43 Those who pay people to sing their praises
    Will find no heavenly reward for their endeavors
    There are others who will not get what they want
    Like those who pretend to be saintly in order to get
        Money. All will burn, *Be sure of God's Truth.*
44 I have set forth my warnings, kinsmen
    To make you wake from slumber
    To make you repent. Do you hear, Muslim friends?
    Everything I have said in this song is true
        As are forgiveness and salvation, *Be sure of God's Truth.*
45 I have finished, kinsmen, hear the Truth
    Take it into your hearts, it is the Truth
    The Truth is what the song is about, hear the Truth
    All of us, let us repent, for anyone who in Truth
        Repents will be saved, *Be sure of God's Truth.*
46 I ask you to accept the *takhmis* and
    The reckoning of the date since the *hijra* of the Prophet
    For mankind will find salvation from him
    I have finished the song and the chronogram's
        Total is *rushdi*, pay attention. *Be sure of God's Truth.*
47 I shall praise the Prophet all my life
    Until the time when I shall die
    Because of him God made forgiveness possible
    Let us give thanks to Him and pray
        For Muhammadu who excelled, *Be sure of God's Truth.*
48 Shehu composed the original version of this song
    Nana translated it into Hausa
    Isa wrote the *takhmis*,
    In Hausa, and the reason was
        To bring this warning, *Be sure of God's Truth.*

Sufi Women

Tawassuli Ga Mata Masu Albarka

A.D. 1837/A.H. 1252–53

LANGUAGE OF ORIGINAL: HAUSA/FULFULDE

SOURCES OF TEXT: HAUSA, BELLO SA'ID'S THESIS, PP. 253–259;
FULFULDE, WAZIRI JUNAIDU (ONE PAGE ONLY)

1 Alhamdulillahi, we thank God,
    We invoke blessings on God's Messenger.

2 We invoke blessings on his family and Companions
    And those who followed them, thus we gain self-respect.

3 We invoke blessings on the Companions of the Prophet
    Who are now sanctified.

4 My aim in this poem is to tell you about Sufis
    To the great ones I bow in reverence.

5 I am mindful of them while I am still alive
    So that they will remember me on the Day of Resurrection.

6 The ascetic women are all sanctified
    For their piety they have been exalted.

7 They prayed ceaselessly to be delivered from the Fires of
      Hell
    Take this to heart, my friends.

8 I have written this poem to assuage my heart:
    I remind you how they yearn for God.

9 I swear by God that I love them all
    In the name of the Prophet the Messenger of God.

10 The scent of their yearning engulfs me
    Its intensity exceeds the perfume of musk.

11 To the Prophet's disciples who draw close to God
    I bring all Muslims to Aisha

12 Aisha, the noble daughter of Al-Siddiq
    The believer, an honest man, Abubakar the esteemed.

13 To Muslim women I speak of Zainabu Jahshi
    I cherish them, Lord of the World.

14 You made her to exceed, according to Aisha,
    She was held in esteem by the Prophet.

15 I speak of all the mothers
    Who were the wives of the Prophet

16 And Faɗima Zahra'u, or Batulu
    Gracious lady, close follower of the Prophet.

17 She was peerless, she who shunned the world,
    The Prophet's daughter, who was better than any other child.

18 I speak of Aminatu Ramliyya
    And Ummu Hassanu, both of Kufa.

19 As was Ummu Sufyanu of Suriyyi
    And the relative of Fudailu, a most kind person.

20 The mother of the Prophet was pious
    A reformer, and upright.

21 I speak of the wives of the Prophet
    For his wives were ascetics.

22 She was very generous and kind
    Daily she gave away gifts: she never ceased.

23 She gave alms most generously
    Undoubtedly she wept day and night.

24 She used to say, "I have no tongue"
    She had no wish to speak.

25 She bought horses for the Jihad of the Lord
    And to follow the Way of the Prophet of God.

26 I speak of Al'umatus Salliyatu
    For her asceticism and also Umayyatu

27 Umma Haruna had radiance
    and Habibatu Adawiyyatu recited the Divine Names.

28 I speak of Rabi'atul Adawiyya
    Who was more pious than anyone else.

29 Adawiyyatu Kaisiyyatu of Basra
    Exalted, able to see the unseen, radiant

30 She had a mastery over learning and exceeded all women
    She was the outstandingly pious person of her time.

31 And so to Ummu Ayyuba of Lansariyyatu
    And Umm Darda'u and Mu'azatu.

32 Her prayer was a thousand prostrations
    Rabi was cognizant by day and by night

33 In order to please the Prophet's heart.
    On the Day of Judgment you will understand her zeal

34 Rabi'atu the daughter of Ismailu

Zealously praying to God
35 She could see male and female jinns
Because of her sainthood and praying to God
36 And Ru'kayyatu of Mausiliyyatu
And Raihanatu Majnunatul the Pious
37 And Sha'awanatu, also pious
And Atika Unawiyyatu Hidatu
38 Aisha, the daughter of Ja'afaru, Ubaidatu
Daughter of Abi Kulaibu, and Ahhiratu
39 Umratu was an ascetic and so was Mu'azatu
Of Mausili, and so too Majidatu.
40 And Maryamu of Basra and Mua'zatu
Maimunatul Majnu'atul akilatu.
41 I speak of Maimunatu Sauda'u
All pious, and Zahara'u.
42 Whose intense piety made her appear transformed;
For when they reached this stage of Sufism they gained
    much.
43 I speak of Faɗimatu Nisaburi
Who was zealous even to those who understand enthusiasm
44 And so to the daughter of Hassan, Nafisatu
Who prostrated herself on account of her piety.
45 She recited the Qur'an six thousand times in the grave
Prayed and fasted: note well her devotion
46 Born at Mecca she was a descendant of the Prophet
She grew up in Medina where she was honored
47 Anyone visiting her grave
And praying there would receive blessings
48 The blessings and compassion of God
Fell upon Egypt on account of Nafisatu
49 I speak of Faɗima, daughter of Abbas Saihatu
Who taught and was a preacher
50 She used to mount the steps outside the mosque and preach
    to women
Her sermons caused them to fear and repent
51 She made an attempt to stop using the steps
But realized that the Prophet had heard of this decision
52 "She is a truly noble person on account of her work"
The Prophet told Tarinu in a dream

53 She set aside considerations of family and possessions
   Choosing instead God and his religion

54 I speak of the ascetic who withdrew from the world
   Fakhriyyatu of Basra, mother of Yusufu

55 She entered into a Sufi state of holiness
   In which she stayed for forty years

56 At the end of her life she went to Mecca
   Where she died and was buried near Hadiza

57 I pray, O God, for their blessings
   Give me the grace to repent my sins.

58 Out of respect for their greatness I dedicate myself
   Believing that I will receive what I request

59 For their majesty will wipe away my sins
   And because of them I will escape the burden of my wrong
      doings.

60 In this world and the next, where souls await judgment
   I will rely on them for my salvation.

61 I know full well that I have committed many sins
   Yet I hope for escape on the Day of Retribution

62 The rest is about the women members of the community of
   Shehu ɗan Fodiyo, for whom I pray

63 I speak of those who are still alive
   And those who have died

64 I mention first of all Shehu ƊDegel, our father
   Ɗan Fodiyo, he is our leader

65 And Iyya Garka who was exceedingly pious
   Giving alms, she completely ignored worldly things

66 Then Inna Garka who was very pious
   Good-natured and generous to her kinfolk

67 I speak of the other wives of the Shehu
   For they were all pious

68 The teacher of women, Habiba
   She was most revered and had great presence

69 I speak of Aisha, a saint
   On account of her asceticism and determination

70 And Joɗa Kowuuri, a Qur'anic scholar
   Who used her scholarship everywhere

71 I speak also of Biada who was diligent
   For her attribute was in reclusion

72 And 'Yar Hindu, daughter of the *Imam*
Who was diligent at solving disputes

73 There were others who were upright
In the community of the *Shehu;* I have not listed them

74 Very many of them had learned the Qur'an by heart
And were exceedingly pious and zealous

75 They never tired of preaching the righteous Faith
Those of the *Shehu* reached as many as a hundred

76 The song which has listed them is now finished
And you now know of their fine reputations

77 May God reunite us with them in the Next World
And through them may we achieve salvation

78 Together with my mother and father and all Muslims
May we be delivered, O Lord of Gifts.

79 For the sake of the glory of him who was exalted
Above all other mortals. My song is finished

80 I thank God Almighty
To whom all prayers are addressed

81 May He bless Ahmadu and all his family
And all those who followed them

82 And his Companions, all of whom were exalted
And the faithful who are enshrined in light

83 The chronogram of the year of the Prophet's *hijra* is
Nabshiru
It is ended, let us say Nabshiru.

written during a siege.

So Verily …

Fa'inna ma'a al-usri yusra

A.D. 1822/A.H. 1238–39

LANGUAGE OF ORIGINAL: FULFULDE
SOURCE OF TEXT: WAZIRI JUNAIDU

1 Lord God Almighty, all Powerful, he who asserts there is
   more
   than one god will perish.
2 One God, Almighty, nothing is perfect except it comes from
   Him.
3 Come to God, receive His generosity: all good things are
   derived from Him.
4 Anyone who says he requires nothing of God is either
   ignorant or an unbeliever.
5 Everyone who seeks God's help will receive it,
   for God allows people to make requests.
6 I pray God will show me the Way of religion and that I will
   keep to it until I die.
7 God is Pure, and forgets nothing: those whom He forgives
   find peace.
8 May He bless us and show us the Path, and may He help us
   to remain one people.
9 We pray for victory and that the rebellion of Ibra may be
   overcome.
10 We pray, too, for forgiveness in this world and the next.
11 Call upon God always, so that things which are too difficult
   may be made easy.
12 Pray to God, do your meditations, praying for forgiveness
   and giving thanks.
13 Look at His generosity! It is unbounded, His munificence is
   infinite.
14 We give thanks to God and pray for our Lord of the Uni
   verse.

In Praise of Ahmada

Kiran Ahmada

A.D. 1839/A.II. 1255

LANGUAGE OF ORIGINAL: HAUSA
SOURCE OF TEXT: WAZIRI JUNAIDU

1 Let us thank the Everlasting God
   Praise be to the King who created Muhammad.
2 Let us for ever invoke blessings and peace
   Upon the Prophet who excels all others, Ahmada.
3 Accept the song of praise I shall sing
   Accept, O people, let us praise Ahmada.
4 God has enjoined us to praise him
   Let us make firm our intention to praise Muhammad.
5 That we might obtain light and radiance of heart
   And be cleansed by praising the Finest One.
6 We beg forgiveness from God who is instant in His Generosity
   May he give it to us because of the rank of Ahmada.
7 We pray for pardon that He might forgive us
   The Munificent King, for the sake of Ahmada.
8 The best of the best, he excels every other in rank
   God himself who said that He has raised Ahmada above all others.
9 The heavens are limitless, but they do not reach
   As high as the glory of Muhammad.
10 The glory of the firmament seems diminished when compared to
   The glory of our Prophet Muhammad.
11 His light exceeds the light of the full moon
   There is no light like the light of Muhammad.
12 As for bravery, no warrior has ever matched the courage shown by Ahmada.
13 Musk and myrrh do not equal
   The perfume emitted by the body of Muhammad.

14 As for his beauty and physique, he surpassed all
    For nowhere is there the like of Muhammad.

15 There has never been created a man like him
    And none will ever be created like Ahmada.

16 As for his wisdom, there is none like him
    Cheerful and smiling was Muhammad.

17 He was never angry. Only sin caused his righteous anger.

18 When he was angry he resisted all attempts
    To persuade him to overlook the offence; only repentance
        would suffice Ahmada.

19 He showed great forbearance toward everyone
    Like the rain cloud in the rainy season was the generosity of
        Muhammad.

20 God enabled him to perform miracles
    The Qur'an is evidence enough of the wonderful powers of
        Muhammad.

21 The dying of the Persian fire is another example
    As is the river of Sawa which dried up because of Ahmada.

22 And the house of Khusrau crumbled until of the Magian
        priests
    One had his dream, and they knew fear of Ahmada.

23 On the thirteenth day the moon split in two
    As recorded by al-Bukhari and al-Tirmidhi in their accounts
        of Muhammad.

24 It was he who uttered and explained the words of the
        Qur'an
    It was a great miracle of the Best of Mankind, Ahmada.

25 On this day the sky bowed down in afternoon prayer
    Because Ali sought help from Muhammad.

26 Asma' the daughter of Abubakar had true understanding of
        him
    Compare him with a lion, the Prophet Muhammad.

27 The very trees and rocks pray for peace
    Upon our Prophet who excels everyone, Ahmada.

28 They prostrate before him so that their Creator will see
    Good news, exceedingly good news, he has recognized
        Muhammad.

29 He it was who was mounted on al-Buraqa on a journey to
        heaven

No other has ascended save the Best of Mankind, Ahmada.

30 He stroked the goat of Umm Mabad and straightaway
On account of his miraculous powers, she gave milk,
Ahmada.

31 He caused clouds to make a shade for the camel
When she brought a complaint to the Prophet Ahmada.

32 The horse of Suraka, because of a miracle, seemed rooted
In the hard rock: all for the high rank of Ahmada.

33 The words of the lizard, in God's name, are proof of the
miraculous powers
And so is the gazelle, for the sake of the Best of Mankind,
Ahmada.

34 "A dove laid an egg," he said and explained
This was one of his miracles, our Prophet Muhammad.

35 He gave Ukasha a stick which was transformed
Into a dagger there in battle, our Prophet Muhammad.

36 This was witnessed by the angels:
Proof of the miracles, Best of Mankind, Ahmada.

37 The small remainder of water left after his ablutions
Was ample for the beasts as well as the army of Ahmada.

38 Likewise the Qurayshi, when they were starving
During the final battle in Mecca, for Ahmada.

39 And the dried well of Hudaibiya
Where water appeared after arrows struck it, for the sake of
Ahmada.

40 The large tree stump wept and sighed
Because it was separated from Ahmada, another miracle.

41 You know they are numerous, uncountable
And Halima saw many of them, Ahmada.

42 God alone knows them all, the One, the All-Knowing
The King who caused the Prophet Ahmada to excel over all
others.

43 O Lord, we pray for delivery from the world
For the sake of his rank, the Best of Mankind, Ahmada.

44 Likewise, O my Lord, for an easy death
For the sake of the majesty of our Prophet Muhammad.

45 And ease in answering Nakiri and Munkari
For the sake of the Best of Mankind, the Messenger
Muhammad.

46 O Lord, we pray for comfort in the grave
   For the sake of the Best of Mankind, our Prophet
      Muhammad.
47 O Lord, we pray for salvation in the hereafter
   On the Day of the Resurrection, for the sake of the Best of
      Mankind, Muhammad.
48 Concerning the weighing on the scales
   May the good deeds prevail, for the sake of the Best of
      Mankind, Ahmada.
49 And the receiving of the paper. God, King, Our Lord
   May it be given to us in the right hand for the sake of
      Ahmada.
50 O Lord, cause us to enter into the salvation of the Prophet
   For the sake of his rank, the Best of Mankind, Ahmada.
51 O my Lord, may we safely cross the bridge over Hell
   For the sake of the majesty of our Prophet Muhammad.
52 O my Lord, give us to drink of the waters of al-Kausara
   The lake of the Best of Mankind, our Prophet Muhammad.
53 O my Lord, save us from the Fire on the Last Day and take
      us
   To the place of peace, Paradise, for the sake of Ahmada.
54 O my Lord, on that Day may we see the face of the Prophet
   For the sake of his rank, the Best of Mankind, Ahmada.
55 O my Lord, may we behold Thy Presence, the Presence of
   The King of the Day of Judgment, for the sake of our
      Prophet Muhammad.

YEARNING FOR THE PROPHET

Begore

N.D.

LANGUAGE OF ORIGINAL: HAUSA
SOURCE OF TEXT: ALHAJI MUHAMMADU MAGAJI

Bismillahi!
1 We thank God for the radiance of the Prophet
   The foremost of all creation, Ahmada.
2 Then He created the universe
   And the Prophets, all with the radiance of Ahmada.
3 He created Adam, the forefather of mankind
   He became man of the very soul of Muhammada
4 I praise Him, and His Omnipotence
   I praise God for Creation and for Muhammada
5 I bless and praise Ahmada
   And also his followers, and the relatives of Muhammada
6 O God, You of Power and Knowledge
   Guide and help me in my praise of Ahmada.
7 Place me in that garden of light and praise
   Where I will find pleasure in the beloved, Muhammada
8 O God, receive my song, may it please
   You, and be acceptable to Muhammada
9 The constant repetition of Muhammada constitutes no flaw
   Because this song is about repeating the name Muhammada
10 Indeed I am aware that these couplets do not match
   But my intention is to keep repeating the name
      Muhammada
11 What I desire above all in my heart
   Is to gain the strength to reach Muhammada
12 Hassan and Hussein were foremost in praise of Muhammad
   I pray to them, because of their rank, that I might see
      Muhammada.
13 About whom I think, who is part of all I know and do
   So I will explain about him, praising Muhammada.

14 Listen to my song about longing for Muhammad
    It will tell you about the life of Lord Muhammada.

Muhammad's Early Life

15 Hasten, countrymen, and hear about
    The noble character and place of honor of Muhammada.
16 You will find out about his Companions and hear about
    The deeds they performed during the time of Muhammada.
17 They defended the Faith, despising the world
    Let us emulate them and thereby follow the ways of
        Muhammada.
18 The truth is that Muhammad exceeded all
    There is loneliness without him and I long for
        Muhammada.
19 God exalted him above all mortals
    Who dwell in the shadow of Ahmada.
20 It is my intention to tell everything
    That happened in the lifetime of Muhammada.
21 So that those who so desire
    Can satisfy their need to praise Muhammada.
22 I begin by listing those it is right to mention
    For they are truly worthy of hearing of Muhammada.
23 In the first rank is the most excellent of *imam*s
    In the history of mankind, he is first, Muhammada.
24 This pre-eminence was sought by Adama
    But the one to whom it was given was Muhammada.
25 He was made Messenger of the Angels
    Verily praise is due to Muhammada.
26 Not one of the prophets who preceded him
    Was the equal of Muhammada.
27 Abraham, our forefather, prayed for Muhammad
    And Jesus was given the good news of Muhammada.
28 Our forefather Adam prayed for him
    Prayers which were accepted on account of the status of
        Ahmada.
29 At his name the firmament ceased to spin
    Therefore let us give due respect to Muhammada.
30 His very soul was purified by God
    Before the time of Moses, the peerless Ahmada.

31 The whole earth was purified
   And sanctified through the grace of Muhammada.
32 The Holy Books told of the coming of a Great Man
   Thus proclaiming the good news of Muhammada.
33 They explained his noble character and grace:
   The prophets knew God's servant Ahmada.
34 To the Messenger of God was given the promise which
   Was given to mankind by God, Muhammada.
35 The good news was spread about the coming of Muhammad
   We thank God we are among the people of Muhammada.
36 The Jews knew and understood everything
   Only envy prevented them from following Muhammada.
37 But this envy rebounded on them
   For God fulfilled Himself through Ahmada.
38 All jinns and spirits
   Proclaimed the news of the peerless Muhammada.
39 He was born of pious parents
   God be praised for the antecedents of Muhammada.
40 From Adam and Eve he was descended
   And Abdullahi and Amina who gave life to Ahmada.
41 They were spotless, as ordained
   Their marriage was guarded by the radiance of Ahmada.
42 The earth which groaned, idol-ridden and dark,
   Was overjoyed with the coming of Muhammada.
43 There was joy in the very hills and streams
   On the eve of Friday, the day of the conception of
        Muhammada.
44 The Devil wept and his people too
   As he frightened them with news of the religion of Ahmada.
45 The Qurayshi clan itself was saying
   Tonight Amina has conceived Ahmada.
46 Even the animals in the wild were pleased
   East and West all were joyous at the coming of
        Muhammada.
47 Scholars said defeat
   In the battle with elephants was avoided because of the
        grace of Muhammada.
48 And so Amina saw the peerless one
   As she gave birth on Monday to Ahmada.

49 It was not women alone who were at the birth
  The angels themselves washed Ahmada.

50 For about three days no one saw him
  The angels were the midwives of Ahmada.

51 On whom the essence of all the prophets streamed
  On that day he was known to mankind, Muhammada.

52 The birds flocked together
  Over the Prophet's mother, singing choruses for her milk to
    flow for Ahmada.

53 Kisra's palace collapsed, the pool dried up
  And the fire of Persia was extinguished because of
    Muhammada.

54 Their rulers, terrified, made frenzied enquiries
  For they knew they would perish in the coming of
    Muhammada.

55 It was in the year of his birth that disaster
  Befell the invaders of Mecca, because of Muhammada.

56 Suwaiba, even before Halima
  Breast-fed him, therefore becoming a Muslim because of
    Muhammada.

57 Women gave birth to females alone in that year
  The exception being Muhammada.

58 The supernatural had no part in his nurture
  No, a human being breast-fed Ahmada.

59 And so it was that God took Halima
  Of the tribe of Sa'ad to Ahmada.

60 And He gave her many blessings
  And a high status because of Muhammada.

61 Indeed all her family became prosperous
  Halima witnessed the miracles of Muhammada.

62 The angels cut all evil from his heart
  In fear Halima restored to his mother Muhammada.

63 It was in his third year that his heart was cut
  Just as Sidiku was born, friend of Muhammada.

64 In the fourth year, some say the sixth, others the tenth
  God gave understanding to Muhammada.

65 When he was six, Amina traveled to her home
  To pay a visit to her family at Medina, together with
    Ahmada.

66 He was four when Halima took him [to his mother], they say,
    Or perhaps she returned him at five years of age, Ahmada.
67 Whilst she was there his mother died
    So Aymani's mother took home Muhammada.
68 When he was seven his paternal grandfather fostered him
    God bless Abu Mudalib for caring for Ahmada.
69 He prayed for rain to end the drought
    And rain fell at Mecca through the merit of Muhammada.
70 He spoke of Saif the son of Zi-Yazin,
    And said he would defend Muhammada.
71 He was eight when his grandfather died
    Then Abu Talib gave instruction to Muhammada.
72 He was faithful in his upbringing in all respects
    Drawing his sword to fight in the name of Muhammada.
73 He patiently shouldered the burden of looking after
        Muhammad
    And allowed no one to behave disrespectfully to Ahmada.
74 He loved him dearly and praised him
    Encouraging people to go to Ahmada.
75 He took him to Basra when he was nine
    Returning when he was ten, Muhammada.
76 When he was eleven all envy
    Anger and resentment were taken from the heart of
        Muhammada.
77 Abu Talib took him to Syria when he was twelve
    Returning when he was thirteen, Ahmada.
78 As they passed through Basra, Bahira'u saw him
    And in a miraculous way advised him to return home with
        Ahmada
79 Bahira'u saw the very hills and trees
    Bowing down before him: the clouds followed in the wake
        of Ahmada
80 When he was twenty-five he married Hadiza
    After his third trip to Syria, Muhammada.
81 For his companions Maisara and Na'duru had witnessed his
        miracles
    And told Hadiza about Ahmada.
82 He was thirty-five years old
    When the Holy Spirits were made known to Ahmada.

83 Next came the birth of his daughter Fatima
The death of Zaidu was keenly felt by Muhammada.

84 He was thirty-eight
When he started to preach and see the light of Ahmada.

85 When he was forty
Plus a day, God sent to Ahmada

86 The Archangel Gabriel,
God sent the Qur'an to Ahmada.

87 Evil was overturned: those who practice it
Will never know even a tenth of the mysteries of Ahmada.

88 The way of saying prayers and ablution was sanctified:
People began to repeat them and follow Muhammada.

89 In the fourth year he began proselytizing.
The eyes of unbelievers were closed because they refused to
respond to Muhammada.

90 In the fifth year they went to Abyssinia
The Negus treated them with consideration, because of
Muhammada.

91 The unbelievers rose against Muhammad
Abu Talib was not converted by Ahmada.

92 But the Hashimite clan supported Muhammad
All except Abu Lahab who did not respond to Ahmada.

93 Abu Jahali cursed the Prophet, which enraged Hamza
Who was converted to Islam and joined Muhammada.

94 Hamza struck down Abu the Heathen
Saying he had heard him slander Ahmada.

95 Who dares move when Hamza is angry?
Thank God for this servant of the Almighty, champion of
Muhammada.

96 It was the conversion of Umaru which opened
The Ka'aba to circumambulation by the followers of
Ahmada.

97 For he said, "Do not hide this religion—broadcast it."
And when this happened no one crossed Ahmada.

98 As Islam gained strength, unbelievers came
With their complaints to the family of Muhammada.

99 They said they would cease trading with Muhammad's family
So God brought about their downfall and prosperity to
Ahmada.

100 In the tenth year Abu Talib died
And also Hadiza, the wife of Ahmada.

101 After that he preached at Daifa
And at Sakifu but they all refused to listen to
Muhammada.

102 On his return he went to Nahilatu where the very spirits
Repented and listened to the preaching of Muhammada.

103 As he addressed his relations who only refuted his words
Six young men of Medina joined Ahmada.

104 They listened to what he said about Islam and embraced it
And took news to Medina of Ahmada.

105 In the twelfth year he journeyed to Heaven
And five prayers a day were instituted by Muhammada.

106 The earth was beautified and blessing reached heavenward
All because of the radiance given by the coming of
Muhammada.

107 In one year when fealty was given at Akaba
Twelve men went to Ahmada.

108 When the next year came they returned
To make a second visit at Akaba to follow Muhammada.

109 There were seventy men and two women
And they all gave their pledge to Muhammada.

110 They said, "We will fight for you
We will defend the property and family of Muhammada."

111 They went on the Hajj
And planned how to kill the enemies of Muhammada.

The Hijra A.H. 1/A.D. 622

112 In the fourteenth year he made his *hijra* to Medina
And his enemies came to destroy Muhammada.

113 He entered a cave with [Abubakar] [June 20, A.D. 622]
No one discovered the hiding place of Ahmada.

114 Surukatu overtook him when the Prophet's horse was
unable to move
He aided Ahmada.

115 In that place it was as dry as dust
And no help except God's—who loved Muhammada.

116 When they got to Huza'u, Ma'abad's mother
Was amazed to see Ahmada.

143

117 Before Muhammad reached Medina, each morning
The citizens were anxiously watching for the arrival of
Muhammada.

118 When they espied him they ran [Rabi'u Lawwal 12, A.H. 1]
Toward him, joy had arrived with Muhammada. [June 28,
A.D. 622]

119 They helped him dismount, fulfilling the promise
They had given to Ahmada.

The Battle of Badr A.H. 2/A.D. 623

120 In the second year of the *Hijra*
He waged war against the enemies of Muhammada.

121 The Commander Abdullahi, son of Jahashu [Rajab A.H. 2]
Led the army against the enemies of Muhammada. [November A.D. 623]

122 In that year the peerless one
Fought Harbo, whose men, though brave, had not the
courage of Muhammada.

123 There were nine hundred
And fifty of the enemy at Badr when they met Ahmada.

124 The Muslims were three hundred and ten
And three, only they were with Ahmada.

125 When they positioned themselves the unbelievers charged
At the men like lions in front of Ahmada.

126 When Aswadu loomed, Hamza enraged
Killed Shaibatu in front of Ahmada.

127 Their leaders were slain, others captured
The Angels of Gabriel were the warriors of Muhammada.

128 Ummayatu and Abu Jahalu were killed
And the glad tidings reached the home of Muhammada.

129 They asked who had won ostrich feathers in his helmet
And heard it was Hamza, uncle of Muhammada.

130 After a three-day battle, he spent the night at Badr
Then went to Medina. Bravo, Ahmada.

131 After that Umaru of Afalahu
Made life difficult for Muslims and Muhammada.

132 The tribe of Kaini'ka'a would not convert
So war was waged against them by Ahmada.

133 'Dan Maslama was killed
When Ka'abu slew him he told Ahmada

134 The tribe of Abu Sufyan failed in their endeavours [A.H. 2]
And the unbelievers became terrified of Muhammada.
[April A.D. 624]

The Battle of Uhud Shauwal A.H. 3/January A.D. 625

135 They came in a great horde
Of three thousand men to fight Muhammada.

136 The unbelievers made preparations on Wednesday and
Thursday
On Friday they advanced to the camp of Muhammada.

137 Sa'adanu and Usaidu kept guard
At the gateway to the hut of Ahmada.

138 On Friday after the afternoon prayer he mounted
And his men formed ranks behind Ahmada.

139 He was in armor
Because a man well prepared was Muhammada.

140 The standards were raised
And carried by Sa'adanu and others who followed
Muhammada.

141 They flanked him to left and right, ready for the battle:
They were gorged with rage at the enemies of
Muhammada.

142 When dawn broke they were at Uhud
Where the unbelievers met with Muhammada.

143 The Muslims made their headquarters at I'nina
To kill the unbelievers who had shunned Ahmada.

144 Look at the ranks of young men
Who, like Hamza, were killed in front of Ahmada.

145 Think that you see Hamza wheeling here and there
As he fought so magnificently for Muhammada.

146 Their weapons, bows and arrows, were at the ready
Their swords drawn: they killed the enemy for Muhammada.

147 On the first clash they defeated them
Give thanks for the noble youths of Muhammada.

148 The peerless one was injured
But Ubaiyu was cleft by the spear of Muhammada.

149 The unbelievers fled the field knowing
     There were no signs of defeat by those with Ahmada.

150 After burying the martyrs killed in battle he turned for
        home
     And Fatima washed the spear of Muhammada.

151 They spent the night cauterizing their wounds
     The following day they pursued the unbelievers, the
        enemies of Ahmada.

152 They reached Hamra'u Uzdu where
     They made a camp: no one could contest with Ahmada.

A.H. 4/A.D. 625

153 In the fourth year they went to Mahunatu [Safar A.H. 4/May
     A.D. 625]
     Which had felt sympathy with the cause of Muhammada.

154 They also raided Raji'u where were
     Many of the enemy including Huzailu who rejected
        Ahmada

155 As for Hasimu he won fame
     By killing seven of the great warriors of the foes of
        Muhammada.

156 In the same year he fought the tribe of Nalir [A.H. 4/June A.D.
     625]
     Jews who had previously made a pact with Muhammada.

157 Which they broke, so he fought them
     And their weapons fell into the hands of Muhammada.

158 Their unreliable leaders broke the pact
     By saying they could conquer Muhammada.

The Second Battle of Badr A.H. 4/February–March A.D. 625

159 The second encounter at Badr was in the same year
     The unbelievers grew afraid of fighting Ahmada.

160 Nu'aimu was therefore instructed
     To cause terror among the companions of Ahmada

161 The men rode out to Badr unafraid and
     They camped for eight days awaiting Ahmada.

162 Their army returned wounded and bereft
     The Muslims returned with booty to Ahmada.

A.H. 5/A.D. 626

163 In year five was the battle of Ruka'u [Muharram A.H. 5/May A.D. 626]
Only the women were left—the men ran rather than face Ahmada.

164 In the same year were fought the tribes of Muraisi [A.H. 5/December A.D. 626]
And the Beni Mus'dalaki led by Muhammada.

165 He killed the men and carried off the women and wealth
For whom they paid ransom to Muhammada.

The Battle of the Trench A.H. 6/February–March A.D. 627

166 He fought the unbelievers at the Battle of the Trench
For they had collected an army to fight Muhammada.

167 The Qurayzah were to the west, the Ga'afanu to the east
They had ten thousand men surrounding Ahmada.

168 The Qurayzah and Ga'afanu and the tribe of Naliru
Had formed an alliance against Muhammada.

169 As Muhammad stepped forth he had no more than three thousand men.
At Salah was the war camp of Muhammada.

170 They stayed there twenty-four days waiting for the battle to commence
They prepared their arrows and swords for Ahmada.

171 When the battle was at its height,
The two Sa'ads took the good news to Ahmada.

172 Abdu Wudiri led his men into battle
Aliyu killed them in front of Ahmada.

173 As he held aloft the head of the warrior he'd killed
Ikirimu fled in fear of Muhammada.

174 Nu'aimu entered into the mercy of God
The peerless one outwitted the enemy of Muhammada.

175 The Prophet sought help and was given it
For he routed the enemy, Ahmada.

176 The angels themselves gave voice to the battle cry, God is Great!
And routed them before returning to Ahmada.

177 When the tribe of Lahazabu fled at night
   He mounted and rode toward the tribe of Qurayzah,
      Muhammada.

178 He made preparations for a period of twenty-five days
   Awaiting their submission to Muhammada.

179 Their refusal meant death to all the young men and their
      leaders
   They were executed in front of Ahmada.

180 That night they were placed in a mass grave [A.H. 5/March
   A.D. 626]
   Sa'adu was in charge of the whole operation, Ahmada.

181 The women and children were sold
   To pay for the cost of the horses and weapons of the Jihad
      of Muhammada.

182 Only one woman was killed
   Then the town was put into proper order with the victory
      of Muhammada

A.H. 6/A.D. 627–628

183 In the sixth year of the *Hijra* [A.H. 6/June A.D. 627]
   War was taken to the tribe of Lahayanu which fled before
      Ahmada.

184 It rained for seven days and nights
   In answer to the prayers of Muhammada.

185 In that year he fought at Akaba
   Where Aku'u's son found favor with Muhammada.

186 He sent Abdullahi to Rafi'u,
   His fractured leg was healed because of Muhammada.

187 The treacherous Rarnawa went to them
   But he treated them like enemies, such was the judgment
      of Muhammada.

188 Then he waged war against Hudebiya
   Who were the drinkers of goat milk, Ahmada.

189 He had then to prepare himself
   For the unbelievers rose up against Ahmada.

190 He was enraged and they cowered with fear
   So they sought to reach agreement with Ahmada.

191 They wanted to settle matters between them
   And he agreed, peace be upon them, Ahmada.

192 In that year he sent messages to
     All kings, instructing them to repent and follow Ahmada.

193 He said they should fear God and obey Muhammad
     If they did not they would become the slaves of
        Muhammada.

194 He sent letters to them all
     Which terrified them: they feared Muhammada.

195 He sent Hadibu to King Kaukisu
     To make him repent and follow Ahmada.

196 Dihiyatu went to King Kaisara
     Who, while refusing to be converted, sent gifts to
        Muhammada.

197 It was Huzafatu's son who went to King Kisra
     Who ripped up the letter, refuting Muhammada.

198 So God brought about his downfall
     And all his territory belonged to Muhammada.

199 Amro was sent to Najasu
     Who was converted and followed Muhammada.

200 Shujahu son of Wahabu went to Harisu
     Who tossed away the letter of Muhammad.

201 Salihu went to Huzatu who said
     He would give allegiance if given eminence by Ahmada.

202 He did not receive this so he refused to convert and died
     God protect us and give us good relations with Ahmada.

A.H. 7/A.D. 628

203 In the seventh year Haibara was conquered
     Listen to what I have to say, Ahmada. [August–September
     A.D. 628]

204 Do not leave me alone, it is not fair, my friends
     Come, join me as I long for Muhammada.

205 Stop finding difficulties where there are none
     And listen to the exploits of Muhammada.

206 Haibara was a major city where a huge number had gathered
     But none were left after clashing with Muhammada.

207 The King of Haibara together with his warriors
     Tasted the spears of the men of Muhammada.

208 The strongest men and all the elders fell
     For their envy had caused them to reject Muhammada.

209 They were killed by Aliyu and Zubairu
Siddiku and Faruku, all mighty warriors of Muhammada.

210 All the young men were executed
And their brides were the captives of Muhammada.

211 Kinanatu was also executed
His wife, Safiyatu, was married to Muhammada.

212 When the Most Excellent One completed everything he
turned for home
His warrior horde causing a cloud of dust to rise,
Muhammada.

213 On their journey home they rested the night
And all failed to rise in time for the prayer, except
Muhammada.

214 In the same year a woman sent Muhammad
A poisonous charm which itself informed him of its nature,
Muhammada.

215 The sun moved back to the late afternoon position
And then fell, a miracle accomplished by God for
Muhammada

216 Asma'u stored all these acts in her memory
So that all would know of the miracles of Ahmada.

217 Then he performed the lesser pilgrimage
Two thousand Muslims accompanied Muhammada.

218 On reaching Mecca the unbelievers were afraid
He went to the Ka'aba and made the circuit, Muhammada.

219 After staying there three days he mounted and turned for
home
Come, assist me, in the name of God to praise
Muhammada.

A.H. 8/A.D. 629

220 In the eighth year he fought Mu'unatu
Where many were killed for the sake of Ahmada. [A.H.
8/September A.D. 629]

221 Zaidu was killed there, and Ja'afaru
And Rawahatu's son, all of them standard-bearers of
Muhammada.

222 Halidu took up the standard and fought
And the men fell in behind him because of Muhammada

223 He then gave command, thanks be to God, for all to come,
   And at the river they were given respite, Muhammada

224 His forces marched against Kudaidu [A.H. 9/January 1, A.D. 630]
   Zubairu was given command of 2,000 men before Ahmada

225 When he was near to Qurayzah he made his camp
   Fear spread among the enemies of Muhammada.

226 He sent word to the Arabs that his kinsmen
   The Muslims should make peace with Ahmada.

227 The tribe of Sulaimamu girded themselves
   And with flags flying they rode to join Ahmada.

228 On that day they assembled together as,
   Fully armed, they surrounded Ahmada.

229 You could see nothing of them save their eyes for
   They had dressed as princes to join Ahmada.

230 When the dust had settled the rocks of Mecca seemed close:
   It was as though they had accompanied Muhammada.

231 When the Prophet's tent was raised, he entered
   And it was there that the enemies of Muhammad were routed.

232 'Dan Tafilu was welcomed along with
   Lubanatu, unbelievers who had previously refused to follow Ahmada.

233 Some of them fled but were later captured
   Like Harbu's son, and their fate was in the hands of Ahmada.

234 He overthrew unbelief that day at Mecca
   Men and women alike repented to Ahmada.

235 The Qurayshi came to know Muhammad Ahmada
   They realized they could do nothing except with Ahmada.

236 He stayed fifteen days there [A.H. 9/January 28, A.D. 630]
   Before making war on Hunaini, Muhammada.

237 He then sent a message to destroy Suwa'a
   Together with Uzza, both should be Islamicized, Ahmada.

238 When the place called Malata had been destroyed he went to Hawazina
   And Sa'kifu, all who had refused to followed Ahmada.

239 When he reached Hunaini, they had allied together. Listen

To what I am telling you about the history of
   Muhammada.

240 Do not leave me by myself, I am serious
   Please go on helping me as I long for Muhammada.

241 The Hawazilu and Sa'kifu were excellent archers
   But for all their fire they had no chance against Ahmada.

242 He routed them all including women and children
   And their wealth was carried to Muhammada.

243 Behold the zeal of the Prophet's warriors: his voice rang out
   And no warrior was the match of Ahmada.

244 When he was on the mount, he called attention to himself
   Saying, "You should know I am the Prophet
   Muhammada."

245 The unbelievers were in their thousands,
   Swords in hand, yet none was able to get near
   Muhammada.

246 After they were defeated, he dispersed them, but their
   wealth he returned to them
   To persuade them to fear God and follow Ahmada.

247 When he had finished apportioning the spoils he per
   formed the lesser pilgrimage Al'umra
   At Medina they were left longing for Muhammada.

248 In the same year he fought Da'ifa [A.H. 9/February A.D. 630]
   And exceeded them by the mighty power of Muhammada.

249 In the ninth year war was taken to Uyainatu
   And after that Tanimawa were beaten, Ahmada. [A.H. 9/
   April A.D. 630]

250 When they reached him he gave them all the booty [A.H. 9/
   February–March A.D. 630]
   Who has the patience of Muhammada?

251 Then the whole populace began to come
   Town by town they entered the religion of Ahmada.

252 Among them were the people of Jibu
   The tribes of Asadin and Kilabu, all followed Ahmada

253 And also the tribes of Baliyya, Dayyu, and Da'iffai
   They came at the same time to follow Muhammada.

254 Next he sent an expedition to
   The tribe of Mu'deleki which heard the news of Ahmada.
   [A.H. 9/May A.D. 630]

255 But the army found that prayer leaders had already been appointed and
They sent the alms tax to Muhammada.

256 After that he sent an expedition to Tabuka after hearing
The Romans were ready to oppose Ahmada.

257 He told them to bring alms and make peace
There were thirty thousand in the army of Muhammada.

258 He went to Syria in the dry season and reached
Tabuka—oh! Listen to what I have to tell you about Ahmada.

259 We never experienced what it was like to fight alongside Muhammad
Only the places are known to us, Ahmada

260 Bring water to refresh me as I faint
Today I am weary, longing so much for Muhammada.

261 On this expedition the Prophet instructed his companions
They experienced the miracles of Ahmada.

262 On his journey many *sura*s of the Qur'an were revealed
And people flocked to Ahmada.

263 His enemies were overcome with grief
Chagrined at the praise bestowed upon Muhammada.

264 He stayed two months at Tabuk where the leading Persians
And Byzantines came to fear Ahmada.

265 He sent Halidu to conquer Daumata, Handaku
Ukaidaru, who was brought captive to Ahmada,

266 Wanted to pay the tax of subservients, but his appeal was rejected
We will see God's face only with the help of Muhammada.

267 Next the kings of Himiyira sent
Letters seeking forgiveness of Ahmada.

268 In that year Abubakar [A.H. 9/March 20, A.D. 631]
Went on the *hajj* for Muhammada.

269 In that year was destroyed
The edifice of the idol there, for Muhammada.

270 Aliyu sent a message to all the places of Mecca
That henceforth no unbelievers could enter the Ka'aba, Muhammada.

271 He ordered the stoning of an adulteress
Who admitted her guilt to Muhammada.

272 In the same year punishment was inflicted upon Uwaimiru
And his wife: who can judge like Muhammada.

273 In the tenth year Halidu was sent [A.H. 10/June A.D. 631]
To persuade the people of Najran to become Muslim,
Ahmada.

274 By the time Najasu had completed his work he had
Ensured many had entered Islam, Muhammada.

275 Any who repented were left alone, the others
Were put to the sword, Ahmada.

276 Those who became Muslims were given mounts
And together with Halidu they returned to Ahmada.

277 The Dinu Hanifa came
Together with Halidu, bringing alms tax to Ahmada.

278 Others including Dawafadi na Nabda and Amiru
Came, but the resisters were killed, Ahmada.

279 In that year the Peerless One [A.H. 10/March 11, A.D. 630]
Made his farewell pilgrimage, Ahmada.

280 Try to visualize the journey he took
Accompanied by so many men, Muhammada.

281 They filled the landscape in uncountable numbers
They came to follow God, and the way of Muhammada.

282 Listen to the din and the hubbub
Hear their voices as they chanted with Ahmada.

283 Repeatedly they gave warning as they circled round the
rock,
Around the holy place they followed Muhammada.

284 He explained to them on that *hajj*
That Islam had been completed in the Path of
Muhammada.

285 In that journey a woman gave birth to a child
Which actually spoke out in happiness, Muhammada.

286 He sent emissaries to Yemen and Azerbaijan
And appointed judges, Muhammada.

287 He sent messages to Jariru at Zulkira
Demanding he repent and end disputing with Ahmada.

288 And so it happened that he submitted to Umaru,
Laid down his arms and entered the religion of Ahmada.

289 The King of Rumu, Farwatau, repented
And sent letters to Muhammada.

290 And Kurci of Wabdi and Waddi and Tanafa'u
Others numbering eleven went to Ahmada.

291 He went to Danma and forgave the men of Baki'u
May God draw us close to him, Muhammada.

292 He planned to send an expedition to Amyaku [Ramalan A.H. 10/A.D. 631]
To revenge the defeat of Zaidu who loved Muhammada.

293 In the same year he became ill and died
Oh, grief indeed overwhelmed Muslims when parted from Ahmada.

294 Ansiyyu and Musailimu
Rose up against Muhammada.

295 The Peerless One sent an expedition to destroy Usamu
Young men were sent, Muhammada.

296 Musailimu was defeated at Yammatu
They met with the warriors of Muhammada

297 Who destroyed the enemy crying, "There is no god but God!"
The battle made a pathway for Muhammada.

298 Well you know that for twelve days
He was sick, then he passed away, Ahmada.

299 Some say fourteen days, others eighteen
When we lay down our lives may we find Muhammada.

300 He was able to continue to pray with the people
Except during the last thirteen days, Ahmada.

301 The people performed seventeen prayer cycles
Without Ahmada.

302 At Lansaru that day they encircled the mosque
For they were afraid of losing Ahmada.

303 He preached to them and of his wisdom
Explaining the whole truth to them, Muhammada.

304 When dying he gave instructions
O God that we might die hearing the admonition of Muhammada.

305 He then told them to gather in Aisha's room
And said they must respect all who had followed Ahmada.

306 Then he ceased speaking
In his pain feel pity for Muhammada.

307 He had been given the choice of the world or Paradise

He chose Paradise—who can match the strength of
character of Muhammada.

308 He gave of his wisdom in the fear of God
Praying until he departed, Ahmada.

309 The Angel Gabriel was three days in attendance
God sent him to be at the side of Muhammada.

310 Muhammad Tukur wrote the poem
And Asma'u translated it into Hausa in love of
Muhammada.

311 I ally myself to him as my father did
And Shaikh Abdulkadir, Ahmada.

312 And Shaikh Rufai and Shaikh Ahmadu Badawi
And Shaikh Dasuki, through them may I see the face of
Muhammada.

313 It is their help we seek in this world and the grave
And also in the Next World, so that we may see Ahmada.

314 God enabled me to write three hundred verses
And eighteen for Muhammada

315 O God, forgive the sins of Asma'u
Because she found the strength to long for Muhammada.

316 You know that the Prophet wipes away all grief
So give us renewed energy to long for Muhammada.

Tamat

The Journey

Fitilago/Waƙar Gewaye

A.D. 1839/A.H. 1255; A.D. 1865/A.H. 1282

LANGUAGE OF ORIGINAL: FULFULDE/HAUSA
SOURCE OF TEXT: WAZIRI JUNAIDU

Chapter 1. Doxology: The Shehu's Preaching Life
Born 1754; began preaching circa 1774

1 Let us thank God, the Almighty, for His generosity.
It suffices us, brethren, let us praise him.

2 Let us invoke His blessing and God's peace upon our
Prophet,
His family, Companions, and all his followers.

3 Now I am going to explain the practice of the Shehu
For you to hear what was done in his time.

4 Usman ɗan Fodiyo, Shehu—the Almighty God
Gave him to us here in Hausaland through His mercy.

5 He brought the True Believers out of ignorance, dispelled
the darkness, and made
Everything clear for us with His light.

6 You should know that he called people to Islam in Ɗegel
And also at Dauran and there at Faru, through his zeal.

7 He turned northward, proselytizing
Until all the people answered his call.

8 He returned home to Ɗegel and then went
On to the Niger, always giving his sermons.

9 The Muslim community accepted his call everywhere,
Those of the east and west, because of his high standing.

10 He overthrew non-Islamic customs and
Established the Muslim law. Let us follow his path.

Chapter 2. Preparation for War 1800–1804

11 He said men should take up their bows and quivers
As well as swords, you hear his command.

12 He said, "Make ready the horses, and firm up your intention
To prepare for the jihad."

13 He sent messages to all the major towns,
   Calling everybody who would listen to him.

14 He said, "Show by your dress who you are and what you
   intend.
   Make up your minds what to do, and be prepared."

Chapter 3. The Shehu's Move to Gudu: Tabkin Kwatto

15 Aliyu Jeɗo went there to Gudu with
   Mahmud Gurdam where they prepared a camp for the
   Shehu.

16 Then Agali came,
   He carried the Shehu's things, and his books.

17 On the twelfth day of the month of Zulki'da [Zulki'da 12, A.H.
   1218]
   Our Shehu made his hijra; [February 21, A.D. 1804]

18 On Thursday he took the road to Kwaren Geza,
   To Demba, and Kalmalo; one after the other.

19 At Farkaji he slept, and at Ruwawari,
   At Gudu God gave him lodging, him and his people.

20 There was a faru tree there, it was his meeting place;
   Beneath it fealty was sworn to him,

21 The Shehu, by all including his relatives
   Everyone resolved to support him.

22 Our Shehu appointed his chief officers,
   Making Ɗan Jeɗo the army commander.

23 He appointed a chief judge and also a law enforcer,
   He appointed them to uphold the laws.

24 Kebbi cooperated in helping the Shehu;
   Moyijo came, he and his kinfolk.

25 Mamman Yiɗi Ladan Kalyero, he also
   Helped in the jihad at the time when he paid homage.

26 The Shehu fought five battles
   At Gudu, all victories due to his blessedness.

27 Yunfa gathered men from everywhere;
   To Gudu they came, where he rounded in anger.

28 There Yunfa was driven away, and all his army
   His horses and their armor were captured when he ran away.

29 As well as the royal drums, umbrella, and other paraphernalia
   They were all taken to the Shehu as spoils of victory.

30 Together with Yunfa's personal effects, his boots and sword,
    Even his kola nuts were found and seized.
31 At the battle of Kwatto, the Haɓe were in disarray. [June 21,
    A.D. 1804]
    They never returned again to attack him at his open en-
    campment.

Chapter 4. Move to Safety in Magabci

32 He left there and he slept at Mali'ba,
    And at Gungune, Inname, and Galoje,
33 At Kaurogo and Ɗingyaɗi, Sifawa and Jareɗi,
    Then at Magabci, that was his route.
34 He sent a force to attack Ɓagarawa and Rikina
    As a result Manuri followed the truth with his people.
35 The Sulluɓawa and all of their relatives helped the Shehu in
    his cause.

Chapter 5. The Journey into Gobir and the Battles There

36 He left there and he camped at Sokoto [October 7, A.D. 1804]
    First he conquered Raɓah.
37 Then Ɗangeɗa as well as Gudawa,
    The people of Rima were dispersed because of his warning.
38 He started out and traveled via Gududu and
    Maitaguwa and Huci.
39 He camped at Makaɗa and Kirare,
    He fought wars because of his determination
40 In Gobir, and returned in good order
    There Mo'i died, his man.
41 Mane was attacked, and there Mammadi
    Found martyrdom as soon as he went there.
42 Mamman Tukur and Agali made their own *hijra* to join
    The Shehu; a time of joy.
43 The countryside was pacified
    And Birnin Konni feared him.
44 He left there and set out for the East,
    To the towns of Gobir, they deferred to him.
45 The king of Adar and Yunfa, the king of Gobir,
    Allied together to fight him.

46 There, they met Shehu at Tsuntsuwa,
    Where God showed the people His might.

47 The Imam Muhammad Sambo, Sa'ada and Riskuwa
    Obtained martyrdom while helping him.

48 So also Zaidu and the son of Farouk,
    Ladan as well as Nadumama, his teachers.

49 Many of the reciters of the Qur'an were killed,
    And also the students among his community.

50 Then he camped at Baura,
    And raids were carried out with utmost zeal.

Chapter 6. Retreat to Safety in Zamfara

51 Then Shehu traveled toward Zamfara, [February A.D. 1805]
    They made peace with him because they feared him.

52 The places that resisted the jihad were all destroyed
    While he was in Remuwa, he was victorious.

53 He left there and settled at Sabon Gari,
    The Muslim community increased in love for him.

54 There Namoda came,
    He too helped the Shehu because he loved him.

55 From there the Shehu's younger brother, Abdullahi Bayero,
        led [April 13, A.D. 1805]
    A campaign against Kebbi and he obtained victory.

56 Among the towns, he even captured Birnin Kebbi
    And Hodi, Chief of Kebbi, ran away.

57 Booty was obtained, even gold,
    And much silver when he ran away.

58 Well done, Bayero; he helped
    The Shehu greatly, in spreading his word.

59 Teaching and composing songs: all of this
    He did, everyone knew how much he helped the Shehu.

60 As Aaron helped his brother Musa,
    So Abdullahi helped his brother, the Shehu.

61 The envious ones did not get the least chance of
    Opposing the Shehu, because Bayero guarded him.

62 May God forgive Bayero, O Lord of
    The Day of Resurrection, so that we may see him.

63 May God give him happiness because of the help

He gave to the Shehu, who was his senior brother.

64 Then Umar of Dallaji was given
The flag to go to Katsina with the Shehu's word.

65 Ɗan Alhaji he also met; they all accepted
The message when they heard it, they knew it would lead to victory.

66 The people of the East all arose with firm intention
Of helping the religious fight; Alwali ran off, defeated.

67 Then they came to the city and the Chief of Kano fled,
Destruction came upon Burumburum.

68 Malam Jamo, Ɗan Zabuwa and Ɗahiru
Malam Jabir, all helped for his sake.

69 With Malam Bakatsine they came in great numbers,
They helped, and they accepted his message.

Chapter 7. Advance on Gwandu: Battle of Alwasa

70 The Shehu left Sabon Gari, and he slept at Bukkuyum,
Bunƙasau, Sadawa, and Falam on his way.

71 And also Gazura Margai; he slept at Bagida,
Then on to Gwandu and the river Samu, that was his route.

72 It was there that his friend that he loved died,
When he was at Zauma they came with the news.

73 He was a merciful man, so the people knew him
He was completely trusted by the Shehu, his man.

74 Umaru of Alƙammu was the Shehu's friend,
The Muslim community knew it.

75 The grief at his death became so great that the Shehu
Preached a sermon to his people about his death.

76 At the end of the month of *Sha'aban* the Shehu entered Gwandu
He remained there through the month of *Ramadan* until the time of the *Id*.

77 Then the Tuaregs gathered under Agunbulu
He offered battle and he was defeated at Alwasa.

78 The community gave battle and Hammadi
Obtained martyrdom shortly after his arrival there.

79 So the men fled,
He alone remained and everybody knows of his valor.

80 Very brave young men were killed,
   Zago, Duwa, and Mujeɗo, during that war.
81 Then the army returned to Gwandu; Agunbulu
   Was filled with fear and terror.
82 They beat the drums, boasting, saying,
   That he was the greatest of men. Satan was deceiving him.
83 God, the Almighty King, overthrew him
   For the sake of the blessedness of the Shehu.
84 A testing time befell the Muslims,
   It was a fever, the community begged the Shehu
85 To pray to God to give them health
   So that they might escape from it, by His mercy.
86 Even the Shehu became ill and the people
   Became frightened because they loved him.

Chapter 8. Victory of Alkalawa, Names of Emirs A.D. 1806–1807

87 Then God restored good health
   To the Shehu, the father of Muslims.
88 The army he sent to Gobir
   Was joined by every man of note.
89 After he had completed the preparations [October 3, A.D. 1808]
   He captured Alkalawa.
90 Then Malam Musa at Zaria
   Was given the task of capturing it, which he did.
91 Borno was defeated and given to Zaki, and Maude to 'Dan
      Goni Mukhtari,
   The Shehu gave them both office because of the help they
      had given him.
92 Sulaiman was given the emirship of Kano,
   Ishaq was given Daura.
93 And Sambo, son of Ashafa who helped him,
   He was given 'Yandoto in Zamfara as his portion.
94 When Bauci was captured it was Yakubu
   To whom it was given by God because of his courage.
95 Also Adamawa was given to Buba Yaro;
   Everyone was given his own share.

96 Larlimu as well as Digimsa,
Were given their share of territory to rule.

97 The Shehu divided responsibility [for the territories]. The
west to his brother;
The eastern part to Bello his son.

98 It was at Gwandu that the *Imam* Zangi died,
And also Kwairanga.

Chapter 9. Sifawa, Sokoto, Death of the Shehu
A.D. 1810–17

99 The Shehu left there [Gwandu] and settled at Sifawa.
Opportunity and prosperity increased.

100 Nupe, Songhai, Yorubaland and Borgu, all
There in the West, were in awe of him.

101 Victory was obtained in every quarter,
The Chief of Gwari was confronted at Illo.

102 When people heard the Shehu's call to religion they all
came
From north, west, east, and south, for his sake.

103 He composed *Tabban Hakika* and
Sitirajo in order to praise God's blessing to him.

104 Then he made preparation for his arrival in his town
Sokoto,
He set out and came, his house was made ready.

105 One Monday he came to Sokoto
And he spent two years there. [A.D. 1815]

106 Then he passed on to the next world, in the month of
Jimada [3 Jimada, A.H. 1232]
It was on the third of the month. [April 20, A.D. 1817]

107 From the beginning of that year he was preaching,
All people knew what he meant.

108 May God forgive him and reunite us
With him in paradise, we pray.

Chapter 10. About Bello's Reign
A.D. 1817

109 Then things became very difficult;
The community selected Bello, his son, to succeed him.

110 At the house of Dan Ashafa, people went
    To pledge allegiance to Bello.

111 He organized a campaign in which Shehu Nuri
    Obtained martyrdom.

112 Revolts became numerous; even Abdulsalam
    At Kware, rebelled, together with his people.

113 Dan Jada as well as Namoda
    Were martyred.

114 He fought the wars of Gobir and Zamfara
    And Kebbi, and all other regions before him.

115 He was just and fair:
    He brought about order through exhortation.

116 He shouldered the burdens of the peasantry,
    Likewise, those of his kinsmen, and the whole community.

117 He built cities and he fought battles,
    So too he built mosques in his city.

118 He protected all the frontier posts,
    The community was organized through his efforts.

119 He established law and preached, so that
    The people should do as he admonished them.

120 He taught religion and Islamic law, as well as medicine,
    And he introduced the reading of *hadith* in the council
        chamber.

121 He bought horses for the jihad as well as
    Shields and swords, dividing them among his kinsfolk.

122 Representatives were appointed to all places,
    In his own city he ruled with justice.

123 He sent men to the frontiers,
    To live there—O listen to his foresight.

124 Some were stationed at Gandi and some were sent
    To Burmi; Fodiyo, his son, went to Gobir.

125 Bello was ill for seven months [Thursday, Rajab 25, A.H. 1235]
    There in Wurno he died, in Rajab, on a Thursday.

126 May God forgive him and may He reunite us with him,
    In Paradise, we pray to Him for His mercy.

127 People gathered and made up their minds,
    Atiku succeeded Bello.

128 May God forgive the Shehu and also Bello,
    And Atiku, his children who were caliphs.

129 May the Peace and blessings of God be forever
    Upon our Prophet and his followers.
130 I thank God and I have completed one hundred verses,
    And you have heard this story
131 I also add some thirty to praise My Lord, the Almighty,
    For His mercy.
132 Asma composed them in Fulfulde,
    And 'Isa translated them into Hausa
133 Rewards come from my kinsmen
    And he is All Powerful and fulfills desires.
134 The chronogram of the *hijra* of our Prophet Muhammad
    Shurafa'u [A.H. 1282/A.D. 1865] let us always thank Him
      for His generosity.

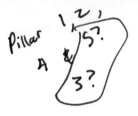

A WARNING, II

Wa'azu

A.D. 1856/A.H. 1273

LANGUAGE OF ORIGINAL: HAUSA
SOURCE OF TEXT: WAZIRI JUNAIDU

1 I give thanks to God the Merciful
    Who created me; the Generous King.
2 He is One, to Him belongs everything,
    He has no beginning because He began everything.
3 He hears, just as He sees:
    He knows all mysteries, He is omniscient and patient.
4 But He does not hear with ears,
    Nor does He see with eyes.
5 Trust in Him and His existence.
    There is no King except God the Bountiful,
6 And trust in Muhammad His Messenger,
    Then you will be an upright Muslim.
7 Do not innovate. Keep strictly to the *Sunna*
    For the *Sunna* will suffice you till you reach Heaven.
8 Repent, for repentance purifies the worshiper
    So he can escape from sin which leads to Hellfire.
9 Safeguard the proprieties of ritual ablution,
    And on the Bridge over the Fire, you will feel no pain.
10 If you are ill, procedures can vary,
    For God gives his servants concessions.
11 What God wants most
    Is work that is willingly done.
12 From God we should all seek
    Forgiveness and His trust.
13 The Everlasting never dies
    Forever and ever and ever He exists.
14 Listen to my warnings, brethren,
    And heed them: admonition is good for you.
15 Let us repent because repentance
    Is the gateway to God the Merciful.

16 Give the alms you must and those you wish, and pray *4*
    For the sake of the Prophet, our Leader.

17 Say your prayer beads in the mornings *2*
    And in the evenings and say extra prayers in the night.

18 To love the Qur'an is to love God:
    For the Prophet's sake, read it constantly.

19 This is the Path of the Almighty.
    He who follows will never turn.

20 Women, a warning. Leave not your homes without good *S?*
    reason
    You may go out to get food or to seek education.

21 In Islam, it is a religious duty to seek knowledge *S?*
    Women may leave their homes freely for this.

22 Repent and behave like respectable married women
    You must obey your husbands' lawful demands.

23 You must dress modestly and be God-fearing.
    Do not imperil yourselves and risk Hellfire.

24 Any woman who refuses, receives no benefit,
    The merciful Lord will give her the reward of the
      damned.

25 I have written this poem of admonition
    For you to put to good use in the community.

26 I end with thanks to God. I invoke His peace
    On the Prophet and his companions.

27 The year of the *Hijra* is 1273.

Lamentation for Aisha, I

Marthiya Aisha

A.D. 1855/A.H. 1272

LANGUAGE OF ORIGINAL: ARABIC

SOURCE OF TEXT: WAZIRI JUNAIDU

In the name of God the Beneficent the Merciful.
God bless the noble Prophet Muhammad.
This is the poem of Asma', daughter of the Shaikh, the Renewer of
the Faith, the light of the times, 'Usman dan Fodiyo, in lamentation of her sister Aisha, the daughter of 'Umar Alƙammu, may God
forgive all their sins and make Heaven their resting place. Amen.

1 To God I make plaint of the kinds of anxieties
   that rest in the gloom of my innermost heart
2 Because of the loss of shaikhs, leaders of the Faith, masters,
   and our brothers, companions of goodness and achievement.
3 The death of the beloved Aisha reminded me of those who
   have passed away
   from among the wise and pious sisters.
4 My sorrows, my loneliness, and my melancholy increase
   the flow of tears on my cheeks into torrents.
5 At the loss of the noble Aisha.
   Oh what a woman! Having all the virtues
6 Of the pious women, humble to their Lord;
   of the women who have memorized the Qu'ran by heart
   and who do extra
7 In prayers, alms-giving, then recitation of the Qu'ran,
   defending the unjustly treated, carrying the burdens of
   many responsibilities.
8 She was a guardian of orphans and widows,
   a pillar of the community, ensuring harmony.
9 I am desolate over losing her, for she was my bosom friend,
   my confidante from our earliest days.

168

10 This is no surprise; the love we had for each other came to us
    from our fathers before us; it was not short-lived.

11 God of Heaven, judge her with pure forgiveness
    and make room for a grave in perpetual light.

12 On the Day of Judgment, preserve her from all that is
    feared,
    from everything terrifying on that day.

13 And place her in Paradise with our Shaikh,
    her father and her husband in the heavenly abodes.

14 Protect all of her descendants
    from the evils of their enemies from every tribe,

15 From the evil of Satan, from the jinn that fights,
    and from every evil thing, secretive and assailing.

16 I shed tears for them but that is in this earthly world;
    in matters of religion our Lord is for them the good
    protector.

17 Blessings and protection upon the Best One, Muhammad
    who hastened
    to inform us of all messages from our Lord

18 And upon his family, his companions, and his followers
    from our community, which is thriving with God's
    permission.

19 When he announced the sign of the times by the *hijra*,
    the Prophet served as your messenger of good tidings.

20 Completed with peace in the year 1272.

LAMENTATION FOR AISHA, II

Marthiya Aisha

N.D.

LANGUAGE OF ORIGINAL: ARABIC
SOURCE OF TEXT: WAZIRI JUNAIDU

In the name of God the Beneficent the Merciful
God bless the noble Prophet Muhammad.
This is the poem of Asma', daughter of our Shaikh 'Uthman ibn
Fudi, in lamentation of her friend and dear one, Aisha, the daughter of Umaru Alƙammu.

1 Oh my eyes weep liberally for my loved one
     as a consolation for my grief and a companion for my
       gloom.
2 Shed copious tears for the loss of Aisha
     the noblest of my dear ones of my age group, my friend.
3 I praise her for her worship, her modesty,
     religion, morals, and glad kindness;
4 For the way she said her *dhikr*, *wird*, and prayer beads
     as well as her reading of the Qur'an. What a dear friend!
5 This poem was written because there is no one else like her
     from among the Brethren. How long my nights dwell on
      her.
6 How often she helped me to forget my own grief
     and how often she helped me most kindly.
7 The depth of my sadness and loneliness after her death has
     grown
     O the multitude of sorrows, the deepening of my gloom!
8 Know you not that love, when firmly established, is priceless?
9 There is no child who could make me forget that love
     and no brother, nothing which could soothe me, not
      even all sorts of riches.
10 Therefore my heart withers from worrying
     sigh after sigh rises up from my grief;

11 Tears have continued to flow constantly
        as if they would never dwindle or cease.

12 As for me, I'm contented with God's judgment;
        I abide by the things I said with regard to the Brethren.

13 It is no sin to make a lamentation
        for Abu Sufyan elegized the Prophet Muhammad after
            his passing.

14 I cry for her with tears of compassion
        and of longing and sympathy for her, and loving friend-
            ship.

15 The Prophet did not prohibit this
        but he prohibited screaming.

16 I pray that God will allay her fears
        and that the Merciful One will provide her with good
            reward,

17 And forgive her lapses and reward her
        for the good things she did for me gladly and graciously.

18 Allow her to meet the Prophet and our Shaikh
        and his famous exemplar, the best of loved ones.

19 May He widen her resting place and grant her entry
        to the highest place in Paradise at the Resurrection.

20 By the glory of the Prophet, the Chosen One, the leader of
        mankind
        May the blessing of God be upon him at every moment.

Praise be to God first and last
Blessings and peace
for our Muhammad
for his family and Companions;
God grant him salvation.

Glossary of Terms

Abbreviations for languages:

Ar. = Arabic
F. = Fulfulde
H. = Hausa

ajami (H.): Non-Arabic texts written in Arabic script; Hausa *ajami* is Hausa written in Arabic script.

al-dhikr (Ar.): See *dhikr.*

Alhaji (Ar.): See *hajj.*

al-kauthar (Ar.): See *kausara.*

alwala (H.): Compulsory washing before prayer, Qur'an 5:6.

amir al-mu'minin (Ar.); in Fulfulde, *lamido juldo;* in Hausa, *sarkin mu-sulmi:* caliph.

aya (Ar.): Verse of the Qur'an.

azumi (H.): The Hausa name for the month of fasting. From Arabic *al-sawm.*

baraka (Ar.): Numinous spiritual quality transmitted by holy people, also spiritual grace.

barzahu (H.), *barzakh* (Ar.): The time after death and before Judgment Day, Qur'an 22:100.

basmala (Ar.): The recitation of the phrase *Bismi 'llah al-Rahman al-Rahim,* "in the name of Allah, the Merciful, the Compassionate."

bidi'a (H.), *bid'a* (Ar.): Innovation introduced into religion.

bori (H.): Spirit possession used as therapy, spread across Africa; *zar* in Egypt, Somalia, and Sudan; *holi* in Niger and Burkina Faso. In Gobir, all women devotees were under the *inna,* sister of the chief.

cazbi (H.): See *tasbaha.*

dhikr, adhkar (Ar.): Remembrance of God, litany.

faqih (Ar.): Jurist, jurisprudent.

al-Fatiha (Ar.): Opening *sura* of the Qur'an, seven verses long.

fiqh (Ar.): Islamic law.

Firdaus, Firdaws (Pers.), *al-Janna* (Ar.): Paradise, Gardens of Eternity, Qur'an 18:31.

Fulani (F.), also Fulbe: Speakers of Fulfulde. Subgroups include Torodbe (F.) or Toronkawa (H.) (the Shehu's clan), Sullabawa, and also the nominally Muslim Bororoje.

Fulfulde (F.): Language spoken by Fulani with marked regional dialects.

gafaka (H.): satchel.

goge (H.): Large fiddle played with a bow; frequently associated with *bori.*

hadith (Ar.): Tradition of the Prophet Muhammad; one of the three cornerstones of the *shari'a,* the others being the Qur'an and *ijma'i* (consensus of learned opinion).

hajj (Ar.): There is a religious obligation which requires all adult Muslims to visit Mecca; this is the *hajj* and it is one of the pillars of Islam. Qur'an 3:96. *Alhaji* or *Hajiya,* a man or woman who has made this pilgrimage.

hakika (H.), *al-haqq* (Ar.): Divine Truth, Sure Reality. *Sura* 69. Also rendered *hakika* (H.).

Hausa (H.): Speakers of the Hausa language, the largest population group to be incorporated into the Sokoto Caliphate.

hijra (Ar.), *hijira,* (H.): Emigration. The Muslim calendar begins with A.D. 622, the date of the Prophet Muhammad's migration from Mecca to Medina, as its base year. The migration of the Shehu from Degel to Gudu in 1804 is referred to as a *hijra.* The word means "break off relations with."

hubbare (F.): Tomb. Derived from *qub* (Ar.). Principally the place where the Shehu lived from 1814 to 1817. He is buried there with four of his children (Muhammad Sambo, Hassan, Asma'u, and Ahmad Rufai) and other principal figures. Visited by the pious. Bello's grave at Wurno is also known as "*hubbare.*"

'ibada (Ar.): Worship, acts of devotion.

ijima' (Ar.): Consensus of legal opinion.

imam (Ar.): Leader of prayer; an essential function of the head of the Muslim community.

inna, iyya (H.): Prior to the *jihad,* titles of women leaders; since the *jihad,* generic terms of respect.

jaji (H.): Literally a caravan leader. Used here to mean a woman appointed to conduct groups of women from their home villages to Asma'u for educational purposes.

al-Janna (Ar.): See *Firdaus.*

jihad (Ar.): Usually translated here to mean the religiously sanctioned war which erupted in 1804 and was led by Shehu Usman dan Fodiyo. The *jihad al-nafs* (struggle against self-will) has importance in the Sufi context.

jinn (Ar.): Spirits, unseen forces.

kafir (Ar.): A non-Muslim, infidel. Used in these texts to refer to the enemy because this is the word used by Asma'u and her contemporaries.

karamat (Ar.): Charisma, miracle, esp. of a saint.

kashf (Ar.): Ability to see the unseeable. Only the most advanced Sufi has the gift to see what is, by the laws of physics, impossible to see.

kausara (H.), *kawthar* (Ar.) or *al-kauthar* (Ar.): Pool (sometimes called "river") of water at gates of Heaven. Qur'an 108:1.

khalwa (Ar.): Retreat from the world.

Kiyama (H.) or *al-Qiyama* (Ar.): The Day of the Resurrection. Qur'an 75:1–40.

laya (H.): Amulet; contains appropriate texts from the Qur'an folded and covered with a soft leather pouch.

madih (Ar.): Panegyric to the Prophet.

magajiya (H.): Traditional title for a ruler's eldest daughter.

mahdi (Ar.): The presager of the end of the world; a future deliverer.

malam (H.): Teacher.

manzuma (H.): The versification of pre-existing prose works.

mu'jiza (Ar.): "The overwhelming." The word has become the technical term for "miracle" and means that any miracle is performed by God.

qadi (Ar.): Judge.

Qadiriyya (Ar.): Sufi order. The Shehu was leader of the Qadiriyya at Degel. Sufi brotherhoods comprise people who adhere to particular ways and follow particular spiritual leaders. The Qadiriyya follow Shaikh Abdulqadir Jelani (lived twelfth cent.). Sufis are seekers of God through discipline, prayer, and mystical practices. Sufism is Islamic mysticism; imparting the knowledge of God to the human spirit.

qasida (Ar.): Praise poem.

quonni (Ar.): Senior jurist; see *faqih*.

ramzi (Ar.): "Abbreviation in writing," coded date.

ribat (Ar.): Walled fortified base built to protect heartlands.

salla (H.): Prayer. The five obligatory daily prayers are said at dawn (*subahi*, H.; *al-subh*, Ar.), 2 P.M. (*azahar*, H.; *al-zuhr*, Ar.), 4 P.M. (*alasar*, H.; *al-asr*, Ar.), sunset (*mangarib*, H.; *al-mangarib*, Ar.), and night (*isha'i*, H.; *al-isha*, Ar.).

sarki (pl. *sarakuna*) (H.): King.

shahada (Ar.): Profession of Faith. "There is no God but Allah and Muhammad is His Messenger."

shari'a (Ar.): Islamic law; different from ecclesiastical law in that it encompasses criminal and civil law and has something to say on all aspects of human behavior.

shaykh, shaikh (Ar.), *shehu* (H.): A leader noted for his learning and scholarship.

sira (Ar.): Literary account of the life of the Prophet Muhammad.

Siradi (H.), *Sirat* (Ar.): Bridge to Paradise, the bridge over which all must pass to their final destiny. Qur'an 8:41.

Sunna (Ar.): The example of the Prophet; "the right path," "the Way."

sura (Ar.): Chapter of the Qur'an.

tadarishi (H.): Stiff covers for holding manuscripts.

tafsir (H.): Qur'anic commentary.

taimama (H.): Substitution of clean, dry sand or earth when water is unavailable for performing ritual ablutions before prayers.

takhmis (Ar.), *tahimisi* (H.): Adding three lines to a couplet to make a verse of five lines. Frequently a pious exercise through which a pupil or disciple honored a master.

tariqa (Ar.): Sufi order or mystical way.

tasbaha (H.): Prayer beads, ninety-nine in number, divided into sets of thirty-three by two larger beads. Prayer sequences (*dhikr*, Ar.; *zikkiri*, H.) are made with the help of the prayer beads. Also *cazbi* or *carbi*.

tawhid (Ar.): Doctrine of the unity of God.

Tibb al-nabi (Ar.): "Medicine of the Prophet"; Qur'anic verses, being the revelations of God, used for medicinal purposes.

Toronkawa (H.): Subclan of Fulani descended from Musa Jakollo, a historical person who migrated from Futa Toro in Senegal to Birnin Konni (north of Sokoto) circa 1200. The ruling elite of Sokoto/Birnin Kebbi is now collectively known as the Toronkawa.

'ulama (Ar.): The body of Islamic scholars in a community.

uwar deji (H.): "Guardian of the royal children," in Gobir. An epithet for the Inna of Gobir used in her praise-songs. This use was transmuted by Maryam, daughter of the Shehu, who succeeded Asma'u as women's leader with the title *uwar deji*.

uwar gari (H.): "Mother of all"; an epithet for the Inna of Gobir, as above. Asma'u was also known as *uwar gari*, but under her the role was completely transformed.

wa'azi (H.): Admonition, warning.

walaya (Ar.): The state of being a saint.

waziri (H.): Officer of an Islamic state with authority next only to that of the caliph. Muhammad Bello's *waziri* was Gidado dan Laima, Asma'u's husband. The place where they lived is Gidadawa, which is near the sultan's palace in Sokoto. The present *waziri*, Dr. Junaidu b. Buhari, is the most famous of the Islamic scholars in Nigeria and beyond; he is a direct descendant of Gidado and Asma'u.

wird (Ar.): Sufi litany of excerpts from the Qur'an, recited for daily prayers.

'yan-taru (H.): Women disciples of Asma'u.

'yan-uwa (H.): Literally "brothers." In the context of these works it means co-religionists, male or female.

zakat (Ar.), *zakka* (H.): Alms tax; charity.

al-zikr (Ar.), *zikkiri* (H.): See *dhikr*.

$\mathscr{N}$otes

1. Nana Asma'u and the Scholarly Islamic Tradition

1. The metaphor of the pearl is utterly appropriate for her, since her nickname was Inji, a term that can be glossed in Hausa as "I hear," or "According to." The speculative explanation for this in her linguistic context is that as a teacher and scholar she was often questioned about issues, and would reply by citing a classical authority on which she could base her answer, thus, "I understand it to be because . . . " or "According to this source . . . " On another level, "Inji" is a woman's nickname in Turkish, perhaps Sufi, contexts. It derives from the Turkish or Kurdish word *inci*, meaning "pearl," and has symbolic associations of purity, chastity, virginity, grace, and feminine qualities, always connected with the sacred. The Qur'ans of prominent Muslim intellectuals in these regions are often decorated with pearls with this symbolism in mind. (Personal communication from Mustafa K. Mirzeler, May 27, 1998.) Since Asma'u was a Sufi of the Qadiriyya order, which had extensive associations with the Turkish cultural context, such a nickname would have been appropriate. "Inji" also suggests the Arabic term *injil*, or "good news."

2. The ethnic origin of these peoples is not clear, but they have been variously described as Torodbe (Fulfulde) or Toronkawa (Hausa). "Fulani" or "Fulbe" is the collective term for those pastoralist and clerical immigrants from the clans of the Futa Toro region in the area now known as Senegal. See also M. G. Smith 1980: 214.

3. The start of his career was in calling the people to religion, which was about A.H. 1188 (A.D. 1774–75) (*Tazyin al-Waraqat,* p. 85).

4. This book is by the Shehu, but the account itself is by his brother Abdullahi. The Shehu incorporated it into his own work *Tanbih al-ikhwan ala ahwal ard al-Sudan,* A.H. 1226 (A.D. 1811).

5. The symbiosis demonstrated between Fulani herders and farmers living in proximity has been addressed in several studies, primary among

them Paul Riesman's *Freedom in Fulani Social Life*. Comparably, relationships between herders and scholars, as well as among various pockets of scholarship in sub-Saharan Africa, are still to be worked out with the help of evidence gathered from further research.

6. *Shehu, shaykh, shaikh,* a Sufi master, a clan head.

7. Insufficient evidence has yet come to light concerning the permanence of marriages in this community. The Shehu married his first cousin, the normal practice, in about 1774. Her name was Maimuna and she bore eleven children, including Asma'u. He also had at the same time three other wives, two of whom outlived him: Aisha, and Hauwa, the mother of Muhammad Bello. Hauwa lived until the 1840s, which meant she was about ninety when she died. Maimuna died circa 1795. The Shehu's fourth wife, Hadija, also died early. We know who his subsequent wives were and the names of their children, but nothing further except "some died and some were divorced," according to Waziri Junaidu. This would seem to indicate that normal family tensions occurred, that sometimes marriages worked and sometimes they did not.

8. This is not to suggest that all Muslims are educated formally, or to a high level, but those who did have access to education followed the format described here. It is important to understand that education is highly valued among Muslims, and the pursuit of education is fostered in many devout Muslim contexts.

9. The Qur'an states that human beings experience the signs of God's mercy in the activities of nature.

10. For a listing of the Shehu's works, see the bibliography of Murray Last, *The Sokoto Caliphate* (London: Longman, 1967).

2. Qadiriyya Sufism

1. Professor P. H. el-Masri in his scholarly introduction to the Shehu's magnum opus *Bayan wujub al-hijra* (*On the Obligation of Migrating*) (1978).

2. Muhammad Bello, *Infaq al-maisur* (*Expenditure/Importance of What Is Available*), circa 1811 (trans. Sidi Sayudi Muhammad and Jean Boyd, circa 1972), p. 7.

3. Gidado dan Laima, *Raud al-jinan,* circa 1840; unpublished Hausa translation, Alkali Sidi Sayudi, circa 1978–80, folio 26.

4. Gidado dan Laima, *Raud al-jinan,* folio 25.

5. The mysteries that are integral to deeper understanding of and involvement in Sufism are indescribable.

6. Abdulqadir was born in the Iranian region of Gilan on the shores of the Caspian Sea. He is an enigma because there is little in his biographies to indicate he intended to create a Sufi brotherhood. He studied

Hanbalite law with Ibn 'Aqil, and received his Sufi robes from al-Mukharrimi, whose school Jelani inherited (Schimmel 1975: 247). So revered is his name that it is presumed to confer unique benefits on all who hear it. His name is chanted in litanies, in India and Pakistan he is eulogized, in North Africa sacred caves are devoted to him, and in popular traditions his name is used to ward off sickness and evil. His tomb in Baghdad is perhaps, after that of the Prophet and those of certain other members of the Prophet's family, the most visited and venerated tomb in Islam, a tomb which "pilgrims from India and Pakistan could, and perhaps still can, be observed sweeping quietly and gently" (Schimmel 1994: 94).

7. By Abd al-Salam ibn Sa'd Sahnun, a Muslim jurist.

8. Some of these messages and poems have survived and been translated. Shaikh al-Mukhtar al-Kunti of Timbuktu was described by the Shehu as an excellent scholar, a refuge, a mediator, and a lamp in the darkness though the two men never met. There is even a popular story still in circulation in the Sudan that the Shehu traveled there to Bara to marry a woman of great piety, only to find she had already married someone else. In fact, the Shehu never made this journey and the story is a myth. Nevertheless, it is interesting that such a liaison would, in the popular mind, have been proper and right and affirmed the clan's connection with the wider sub-Saharan Sufi community.

9. " . . . the literary production of nineteenth-century Sudan is several hundred percent greater in volume than that of the centuries before" (O'Fahey 1993: 21–35). See also O'Fahey and Hunwick, *Arabic Literature of the Sudan to 1898* (forthcoming).

10. *'Arf al-raihan* by Waziri Junaidu (trans. Jean Boyd) describes the lives and work of the illustrious children of the Shehu.

11. *Al-kashf. Wa'l bayan 'an ba'd ahwal al-sayyid Muhammad Bello, 1838–39,* unpublished Hausa translation by Alkali Sidi Sayudi, circa 1978.

12. Abdul Wahab ibn Shir'ani, *Lawkifua anwarifi dabakatil ahayari.*

13. Hiskett 1975: 2.

14. Hiskett 1975: 3.

15. Hiskett 1975: 18.

16. Mervyn Hiskett says that Asma'u "is also credited with a versification bearing the Arabic title *Qasida fi'l munaja,* a work of little literary interest that merely recites the titles of Koranic *suras* or chapters and is supposed to protect the reciter from misfortune" (1975: 44).

17. Brenner 1988: 33–52.

18. Batran 1979: 138.

19. This citation is from Batran 1979: 139–140. Late-twentieth-

183

century critiques of Sufism condemn the idea of sainthood. See "The Izalah Movement and Islamic Intellectual Discourse in Northern Nigeria," Yandaki 1997: 46, and Gumi 1992: 36.

3. The Caliphate Community

1. Arabic script is written in consonants, with dots and dashes added to indicate vowels where they are needed for clarification.

2. Abdullahi Fodiyo, *Al-niyyat fi'l a'mal al-dunyawiyya wa'l-diniyya,* translated into Hausa by Muhammad Isa, p. 9.

3. Abdullahi Fodiyo, *Al-tibyan li huqua al-ikhwan,* 1827. This is a reference to Qur'an 66:6.

4. Boyd and Mack 1997: 205, Poem 30.

5. Hugh Clapperton was witness to the Caliphate community at this time. See Clapperton 1829: 214.

6. This is a quotation at the end of her long work *Medicine of the Prophet* and is dated November 3, 1839. (See appendix.)

7. Boyd and Mack 1997: 331, Poem 60, v. 204.

8. See Boyd and Mack 1997: 248–249.

9. *A Contribution to the History of the Sudan* (*Infaq al-maisur surat al-ikhlas*), by Muhammad Bello, p. 46.

4. The Poetic Tradition

1. Hiskett 1993: 11.

2. In January 1997, after the death of the famous scholar Waziri Junaidu, his heirs made a similar decision.

3. The reader is referred to Mervyn Hiskett's classic work *A History of Hausa Islamic Verse* (1975) for a more detailed explanation of these terms.

4. Because this volume deals with Asma'u's works in English translation only, much of the richness of her poetry is beyond the range of this discussion. Those who are able to analyze her materials in their original forms will find a great deal more complexity and skill than can be accounted for here.

5. The Shehu also wrote a sermon on the fear of Hell, which is incorporated in *A Contribution to the History of the Sudan* (*Infaq al-maisur surat al-ikhlas*), by his son Muhammad Bello.

6. *Takhmis* also can be created by adding one line at the beginning of an existing four; for more on the *takhmis,* see Hiskett 1975: 173–175.

7. See Schimmel 1994: 115 and passim for more on this perspective.

8. The technique would be considered close to plagiarism in the Western literary mode, where ownership of a poetic work is assumed to belong to the first author. The more generous, communal access to poetry

within the Arabic poetic context reflects a different cultural ethos as well as different literary perspectives.

9. Although the Shehu had long been dead, Asma'u speaks of him as though he were alive, reasoning that his spirit continues to be the guiding force of the Caliphate.

10. Asma'u's credibility among scholars as far away as Mauritania is evident in letters to her from them. See Boyd and Mack 1997: 282–283 for examples of this.

5. Sokoto as Medina

1. The other guiding principle is following what is contained in the Qur'an. This dual mandate is discussed further in chapter 1 in this volume.

2. The Prophet Muhammad (A.D. 570–632) lived in Mecca and Medina; Shehu Usman dan Fodiyo (A.D. 1754–1817) lived in what is now northwestern Nigeria.

3. Principally in *The Story of the Shehu, In Praise of Ahmada,* and *The Battle of Gawakuke,* in Boyd and Mack 1997.

4. These include works by the Shehu's son Bello and brother Abdullahi.

5. Al-Maghribi (d. A.D. 1264) is credited with the first such biography of the Prophet. This and other early works have been lost, but their existence is acknowledged by those who credited them as models for their own such creations (Arberry 1965: 64).

6. Al-Busiri's biographers reported that *The Mantle* (*Burda*) was composed when he was partially paralyzed. Having completed it, the poet prayed to God for his recovery, whereupon the Prophet appeared in a dream, laid his hand upon his forehead, and draped his mantle (*burda*) around him. When al-Busiri awoke, his paralysis had lessened and he was able to get up and walk. The story of his recovery rapidly spread and did much to enhance the celebrity of the poem, to which miraculous powers have been ascribed ever since.

7. For more on *takhmis* see chapter 4 in this volume.

8. It has found its way into modern anthologies; see Furniss's translation of *Ma'ama'are* (1996) and commentary on it (1996: 442).

9. "Muhammadu Tukur [a holy man from Zamfara who wrote fierce verse about Hell Fire], was a pupil of the Shehu Usuman dan Fodio; but he came already possessed of much knowledge. Then he increased his knowledge from the Shehu" (Hiskett 1973: 32, citing oral traditon from Alhaji Malam Sayudi, of Katsina).

10. First the call to religion by the Prophet, who made a *hijra,* then

the Battle of Badr, which was won against all odds. This was followed by the Battle of Uhud, marked by the desertion of key troops, then the Battle of the Trench, the focus of which was the dry moat or *handak*. Peace overtures made by the enemy led the Prophet to send out messages to kings to follow him. Whole populations complied, and the Prophet continued to preach to the end of his life. He died at the age of sixty-three.

11. These variants are based on the Arabic root radical HMD, meaning "praise." For more on this the reader is referred to Hiskett 1993 and Schimmel 1992.

12. There are twelve categories of angels in the Qur'an, twelve *imam*s of the Shia with relationships to the twelve zodiacal signs (see Schimmel 1994: 80–81).

13. Abdullahi dan Fodiyo, *Tazyin al Waraqat*, p. 100.

14. To illustrate the way in which allusions were made, compare a poem by the Shehu: "When [the Prophet] made his hijra he journeyed north, and that is the direction I also took. / He fought five battles before they descended in force. I too fought five battles whilst the enemy were still dithering about what to do" (*Munasaba*, vv. 8, 14).

15. Asma'u's uncle Abdullahi wrote an account of this battle, including the line "I was left in the rear calling out, 'O return'" (*Tazyin al Waraqat*, p. 120). This very clearly mirrors the words of the Qur'an:

> Behold ye were climbing up
> The high ground, without even
> Casting a side glance
> At anyone, and the Apostle
> In your rear was calling you
> Back. (3:153)

16. How many of the Prophets
   Fought [in God's way],
   And with them [fought]
   Large bands of godly men?
   But they never lost heart
   If they met with disaster
   In God's way, nor did
   They weaken [in will]
   Nor give in. And God
   Loves those who are
   Firm and steadfast. (3:146)

6. Caliphate Women's Participation in the Community

1. Women scholars are evident everywhere: in Sokoto, Katsina, Kano, and surrounding towns. In every case the women who write and teach model themselves on Nana Asma'u, citing her as their exemplar.

2. These women students often were younger, with childbearing obligations that precluded their attending public classes, while others might simply have preferred to live confined to the home, rather than going out in public. Caliphate women were not restricted to one particular role, but could alternate between being students and teachers, secluded and mobile, according to changing conditions of social position, age, and talents.

3. Examples of such itinerant teachers and of women writers supported and nurtured by creative writing clubs have been described in several contemporary studies, notably those of Furniss, Mack, and Sule and Starratt (see bibliography).

4. His full name is Abu Hamid Muhammad ibn Muhammad al-Tusi al-Shafi'i al-Ghazali.

5. Al-Ghazali is cited in the Shehu's *Bayan wujub;* Asma'u studied the Shehu's works, and learned directly from him, so she had to have been familiar with al-Ghazali, who is one of the most famous theologians in Islamic history.

6. Haroun al-Rashid Adamu quoted in "*Kulle* [Purdah] Among the Muslims in the Northern States of Nigeria," Isa A. Abba, postgraduate seminar paper, Bayero University, Kano, Nigeria, 1979, p. 2.

7. Nur al-Albab, quoted in T. Hodgkin, *Nigerian Perspective,* p. 195. See also the interview with the former governor of Sokoto, Shehu Kangiwa, where he said, "99% of men would like to be in total control of the woman. She is supposed to be in the house looking after the children, they are not even expected to come out." *New Times* 2, no. 26 (April 1981): 40.

8. Boyd and Mack 1997: 70–71.

9. For evidence of this connection, and more on the topic, see Boyd and Mack 1997: 68–82.

10. The Shehu's second and third wives, Aisha and Hauwa.

11. The precise number of her elegies depends on how one counts poems within poems.

12. Even today the family tradition is still carried out at the Sultan's house in Sokoto, which was first built by Fadima's brother Muhammad Bello. The kitchens are busy during the day producing steaming pots of staple foods which are carried to the gates at sundown.

13. Known in Sokoto today as *al-huta*.
14. Trimingham 1980: 47.
15. Bovin 1983: 66–103.
16. Schildkrout 1982.

Works Cited

Abba, Isa. "*Kulle* [Purdah] Among the Muslims in the Northern States of Nigeria." Postgraduate Seminar Paper. Bayero University, Kano, Nigeria, 1979.

Arberry, A. J. *Arabic Poetry*. Cambridge: Cambridge University Press, 1965.

Batran, A. A. "The Kunta: Sidi al Mukhtar al Kunti and the Office of Shaykh al Tariqa'l-Qadiriyya." In *Studies in West African Islamic History*, ed. J. R. Willis, pp. 113–146. London: Frank Cass, 1979.

Bovin, M. "Muslim Women in the Periphery: The West African Sahel." In *Women in Islamic Societies*, ed. B. Utas, pp. 66–103. London: Curzon Press, 1983.

Boyd, Jean, and Beverly B. Mack. *The Collected Works of Nana Asma'u, 1793–1864*. Ann Arbor: Michigan State University Press, 1997.

Brenner, Louis. "Concepts of *Tariqa* in West Africa: The Case of the Qadiriyya." In *Charisma and Brotherhood in African Islam*, ed. Donal B. Cruise O'Brien and Christian Coulon, pp. 33–52. Oxford: Clarendon Press, 1988.

Chodiewicz, M. "Female Sainthood in Islam." *Sufi* 21 (Spring 1994): 12–26.

Clapperton, Hugh. *Journal of a Second Expedition into the Interior of Africa*. Philadelphia: Carey, Lea and Carey, 1829.

Coulon, Christian. "Women, Islam, and *Baraka*." In *Charisma and Brotherhood in African Islam*, ed. Donal B. Cruise O'Brien and Christian Coulon, pp. 113–134. Oxford: Clarendon Press, 1988.

Doi, Abdurrahman. "The Ethical Foundations of the Sokoto Caliphate." Paper presented at seminar on the Life and Times of Amir al-Muminin Muhammad Bello. University of Sokoto, April 1985.

Esposito, John. *Islam: The Straight Path*. New York: Oxford University Press, 1991.

Furniss, Graham. *Poetry, Prose, and Popular Culture in Hausa*. Edinburgh: Edinburgh University Press, 1996.

189

Furniss, Graham, trans. "*Ma'ama'are*" by Isa ibn Shehu. In *Qasida Poetry in Islamic Asia and Africa*, vol. 1, ed. S. Sperl and C. Shackle, and vol. 2, p. 442. Leiden: Brill, 1996.

Gumi, Shehu Abubakar, with I. Tsiga. *Where I Stand.* Ibadan, Nigeria: Spectrum Books, 1992.

Hiskett, Mervyn. *A History of Hausa Islamic Verse.* London: SOAS, University of London Press, 1975.

———. *Some to Mecca Turn to Pray.* St. Albans: Claridge Press, 1993.

———. *The Sword of Truth.* Oxford: Oxford University Press, 1973.

Hodgkin, T. *Nigerian Perspectives.* Oxford: Oxford University Press, 1960.

Kangiwa, Shehu. "The Sacrifices We Make for Producing the President." *New Times* 2, no. 26 (April 1981): 36–45.

Karrar, Ali Salih. *The Sufi Brotherhoods in the Sudan.* London: C. Hurst, 1992.

Mack, Beverly. "Songs from Silence: Hausa Women's Oral Poetry." In *"Ngambika": Studies of Women in African Literature,* ed. Carol Boyce Davies and Anne Adams Graves, pp. 181–190. Trenton, N.J.: Africa World Press, 1986.

———. "*Wakokin Mata:* Hausa Women's Oral Poetry." Ph.D. diss., University of Wisconsin–Madison, 1981.

O'Fahey, R. S. "Islamic Hegemonies in the Sudan." In *Muslim Identity and Social Change in Sub-Saharan Africa,* ed. Louis Brenner. Bloomington: Indiana University Press, 1993.

O'Fahey, R. S., and John Hunwick, eds. *Arabic Literature of the Sudan to 1898.* In the Arabic Literature of Africa series. Leiden, N.Y.: Brill, forthcoming.

Reisman, Paul. *Freedom in Fulani Social Life.* Chicago: University of Chicago Press, 1977.

Schildkrout, Enid. "Dependence and Autonomy: The Economic Activities of Secluded Hausa Women in Kano, Nigeria." In *Women and Work in Africa,* ed. Edna Bay, pp. 55–81. Boulder, Colo.: Westview Press, 1982.

Schimmel, Annemarie. *Deciphering the Signs of God.* Albany: State University of New York Press, 1994.

———. *Mystical Dimensions of Islam.* Chapel Hill: University of North Carolina Press, 1975.

Smith, M. G. "The Jihad of Shehu Usman dan Fodio." In *Islam in Tropical Africa,* ed. I. M. Lewis, pp. 213–225. Bloomington: Indiana University Press, 1980.

Sule, Balarabe, and Priscilla Starratt. "Islamic Leadership Positions for Women in Contemporary Kano Society." In *Hausa Women in the*

Twentieth Century, ed. Catherine Coles and Beverly B. Mack, pp. 29–49. Madison: University of Wisconsin Press, 1991.

Trimingham, J. Spencer. *The Influence of Islam upon Africa.* New York: Longman, 1980.

Yandaki, Aminu I. "The Izalah Movement and Islamic Intellectual Discourse in Northern Nigeria." In *Islam and the History of Learning in Katsina,* ed. Ismaila Tsiga and Abdalla Adamu. Ibadan, Nigeria: Spectrum Books, 1997.

Sources in Arabic

Abdul Wahab ibn Shirani. *Lawakifu Anwarifi Dabakatil Aharyari.*

Abdullahi Fodiyo. *Diya al-hukkam (Light of Judges),* 1806–1807.

———. *al-niyyat fi'l a'mal al-dunyawiyya wa'l-diniyya.*

———. *Tazyin al-Waraqat.*

———. *al-tibyan li huqua al-ikhwan,* circa 1827.

Gidado dan Laima. *al-Kashf. Wa'l bayan 'an ba'd ahwal al-sayyid Muhammad Bello, 1838–39.*

———. *Raud al-jinan,* circa 1840.

Junaidu, Waziri. *Arf al-raihan.* n.d. (Unpublished Hausa translation), circa 1974.

Muhammad Bello. *Infaq al-maisur surat al-ikhlas (A Contribution to the History of the Sudan),* circa A.D. 1811.

Usman dan Fodiyo, Shehu. *Bayan wujub al-hijira (On the Obligation of Migrating),* 1806.

———. *Kitab ulum al-mu'amala (The Book of the Sciences of Behavior).*

———. *Munasaba.*

———. *Tanbih al-ikhwan ala ahwal ard al Sudan* 1226 (1811 C.E.).

———. *Usul ad-din (The Roots of Religion).*

Index

Abbasids, 37–38

Abd al-Salam ibn Sa'd Sahnun, 181*n.7*

Abdullahi, 8, 33; elegy for, 86; in organization of Caliphate, 37–38; poetry of, 64; at Tabkin Kwatto, 69; writings of, 184*n.15*

Abdullahi ibn Muhammad, poetry of, 53

Abdulqadir, 27

Acrostic technique, 49–50, 52

'Adawiyah, Habiba, 84

Afterlife, Sufi beliefs about, 52–56. *See also Fear This*

Aisha, 47; marriage to Bello, 34

Aisha (wife of Shehu Usman), 180*n.7*

Aisha (wife of Sidi al-Mukhtar), 19

Aliyu (son of Dije), named caliph, 36

Aliyu ibn Abdullahi, translation of *The Qur'an*, 24

Alkalawa, Battle of, 33, 72–73, 162–163

Alwasa, Battle of, 161–162

Angels, categories of, 184*n.12*

'Aqil, Ibn, 181*n.6*

Arabic: Asma'u's knowledge of, 12; language conventions for, xix; literary works in, xiii, 21; poetic tradition in, 46–62; script for, 182*n.1*

Asma bint Abubakar, historical significance of, 7

Asma'u, Nana, ix, xii–xiii, 8; appointed leader of women, 34; childhood household of, 10; credibility of, 183*n.10*; death of, 13; education of, 48; elegies of, 27–28; first book, 11; genealogical charts for, 6–7, 8*f*; historical setting for, 2–4; household responsibilities of, 48–49; Islamic education of, 7–8; languages of, xiii, 12, 46; marriage of, 11; personal jihad of, 6; perspective on Islam, 20; poetry of, 10, 49–62 (*see also specific works*); public activities of, 1; renown of, 13–14; role in Sokoto Caliphate, 30–45; as role model, xiv–xv; and scholarly Islamic tradition, 1–14; Sokoto jihad and, 6; translations of works, 182*n.4*; unifying role of, 12; women trained by, 11–12; work of, 12–14

al Badawi, Shaikh Ahmad, elegy for, 28

Badr: Battle of, 69–70, 184*n.10*; in *Yearning for the Prophet*, 144–145; Battle of (second), in *Yearning for the Prophet*, 146–147; Mohammad's victory at, x

al-Bakka'i, Sidi Ahmed, 19

Bashir, Alhaji, 52

Battle of Alkalawa, 72–73, 162–163

Battle of Alwasa, 161–162

Index

Beverly B. Mack is Associate Professor of African Studies at the University of Kansas. She is co-editor (with Catherine Coles) of *Hausa Women in the Twentieth Century* and co-author (with Jean Boyd) of *The Collected Works of Nana Asma'u, 1793-1864*.

❈

Jean Boyd is former Principal Research Fellow of the Sokoto History Bureau and Research Associate of the School of Oriental and African Studies of the University of London. She is author of *The Caliph's Sister* and *Sultan Siddiq Abubakar III*.